W9-CZX-877

PRELOGICAL EXPERIENCE

Prelogical Experience

An Inquiry into Dreams & Other Creative Processes

EDWARD S. TAUBER, M.D.

and MAURICE R. GREEN, M.D.

Basic Books, Inc.   New York

1959

© 1959 by Basic Books, Inc.

LIBRARY OF CONGRESS CATALOG CARD NUMBER 59–8113

MANUFACTURED IN THE UNITED STATES OF AMERICA

DESIGNED BY GUY FLEMING

Contents

Introduction

THE HISTORY OF PSYCHOANALYSIS, beginning with Freud, has been marked by recurring appraisals of its scientific status. Unfortunately, the emotional climate of most of these inquiries has not been conducive to a constructive evaluation of the psychoanalytic approach. Nor has it encouraged the development of methods for realizing the full potentialities of psychoanalysis in the understanding of man and the cure of his illnesses. There are those who devote their energies to the defense of Freud as if it were essential to establish that everything he did was beyond criticism. Such detailed devotion only obscures the vastness of his originality and creativeness. There are others who dismiss Freud's contribution as a myth, perhaps even a huge hoax, without scientific meaning or value.

Physics, the science that deals with laws and properties of matter and energy, often has been used as a model in determining whether psychoanalysis is a science or not. In contrast to the strictly public and operational formulation of theories of physics, the formulations of psychoanalytic theory contain much more of the relatively private experience of the observers participating in the scientific inquiry. Furthermore, this scientific inquiry by its very nature does not readily lend itself to objective verification.[1]

There is no question that much of psychoanalytic theory, and particularly the verification of findings, has presented a challenge to all earnest students of psychoanalysis, for in studying man everything cannot be reduced to purely objective, self-evident terms as in studying the physical world. But when the controversial issues are dispassionately examined, it is recognized that, while psychoanalysis is not a paragon of scientific method, neither is it completely unscientific. Certainly it has contributed a wealth of important material on human motivation, perhaps more than any other psychological discipline. The status one assigns to it, therefore, may depend upon how one defines science.[2]

1] It is interesting to note, however, that even in physics in recent years there has been a trend away from the earlier positivistic position toward a broader position that includes indirection—a widening of the logical gap between observations and basic concepts or laws. Science is often enabled to proceed in a productive, explanatory, and predictive fashion by first setting up fictitious concepts rather than those fully definable by observables. Thus, even in physics, there is a metaphoric vocabulary that is legitimate during the early phases of concept formation.

2] In this connection, see Jerome Richfield, "On the Scientific Status of Psychoanalysis," *Scientific Monthly,* 1954, No. 5, pp. 306–309, for a report on the criticisms leveled at psychoanalysis by a symposium of scientists in psychoanalysis and related disciplines held in 1953 for the purpose of examining the present status of psychoanalysis and its relation to scientific method. Dr. Richfield takes up each of these criticisms and shows that, although some of them reveal inadequacies in the structure of psychoanalysis, most of the objections are not seriously grounded. He is able to indicate quite convincingly that, if one approaches the matter by first identifying what is meant by science, then what occurs in psychoanalysis can to some extent be seen to fit this conception.

Introduction

Many of the processes in psychoanalytic procedure deal with types of experience which have so far not lent themselves to the model of the physical sciences and perhaps will never do so. Quite possibly, even, more is lost than gained by attempting to force them into the conventional scientific mold. The major effort, we believe, should be directed instead toward examining psychoanalysis in terms of its own proper set of principles and goals, to determine whether it is achieving what it sets out to do as fully and fruitfully as possible.

With this end in view it is our intention now to re-examine something of the foundations of symbolic theory and to consider the possibilities of a more effective approach in this field. Specifically we shall explore aspects of symbolism in relation to the vast continuum of more or less diffuse referential processes that operate at the margin of awareness and *come* to the edge of focal attention rather than being divulged through the logical formulations of the conscious mind. These prelogical forms of thinking—the dream, the daydream, the extrasensory perception, the insight, the creative inspiration, the hunch—have so far received scant attention in symbolic theory for reason of the fact that they do not operate in the logical mode. Their language is not the conventional language of speech, but the nuances, tones, and subtle gestures of the unconscious processes.

Our general thesis will be that these prelogical processes are an inherent part of man's symbolizing equipment and that they illuminate and present his inner experience of himself and his relation to others in a far wider sense than is attributed to them in current psychoanalytic theory or realized in the procedures at present employed in psychoanalytic practice. We shall propose that a broader concept of symbolism is needed, one that takes cognizance of these processes as forms of interpersonal communication, and that novel methods must be devised for utilizing them, as well as the spoken word, as an entree to the unconscious in the therapeutic situation. Only then, we believe, can dream interpretation or dream analysis become the truly effective therapeutic tool that it is capable of being.

In setting ourselves the task of exploring the prelogical processes, however, we must not lead the reader to assume that we regard the logical modes of experience as unimportant in the human situation. Needless to say, both the logical and the nonlogical are given data in every experiment in living. Both are intimately concerned with man's existential dichotomy—the human paradox of separateness and togetherness. The prelogical mode of thinking and feeling brings man into emotive relationship with his fellow man by intuitive processes that operate below the level of awareness. The logical mode allows the fruits of this togetherness to be expressed in the forms of communication conventionally employed in his conscious interaction with others. The confluence of these two modes of experience occupies the clinician every moment of his working day. Thus perhaps psychoanalysis, by its very nature, is more stubbornly involved in their meeting than any other occupational enterprise.

Nevertheless we shall focus our attention on the prelogical processes. To understand man and cure his illnesses we must understand not only what he tells us about himself in the logical forms of conscious communication, but also what he tells us in the subtle forms of communication that operate below the levels of awareness. Yet current symbolic theory curiously neglects this very important aspect of inter-personal activity. It assumes that the only valid approach to scientific investigation is through the logical processes. We shall propose that a quite different approach may be the truly scientific approach to a study of man's mind. As we see it, the analogical approach is not only eminently correct, but absolutely essential to the proper picturing of certain types of psychological material, including dream material. In fact, the central point of this book is to demonstrate that analogy, metaphor, intuition, guesses, hunches, and spon-taneity, when properly used, have an extraordinarily im-portant contribution to make both to the scientific structure of psychoanalytic dream interpretation and to the thera-peutic aspect of psychoanalysis. Such devices must, of course, be used warily. But the attitude of extreme caution which the modern scientist often directs toward them is crippling and tends to reduce the fertility of psychoanalytic procedure.

1

The Prelogical Processes in Human Experience

MAN as a psychobiological unit is related to the world about him, in all its animate and inanimate forms, in a much more extensive way than his awareness permits in terms of his own symbolic formulations of experience. The interpersonal theory of personality alludes to this idea in the following statement: The self is a selective limiting aspect of experience which registers only a portion of the informational intake. What the human being consciously reveals of himself to the outside world and to himself is a very small part of what he has experienced. His experience can be likened to a vast waterfall, but his recognition and projection of such experience is funneled down to a mere stream through the excluding devices.

Psychically, man is constantly registering a huge manifold of percepts which never enter awareness as conscious knowledge, as demonstrated by recent investigations into

I

the perceptual activity of the mind at subthreshold levels of awareness. The results of these investigations also strongly suggest that below the levels of awareness, the prelogical processes go on night and day. The prelogical processes build out of the innumerable subthreshold percepts the foundations of one's everyday thinking, relating man to the world about him in many subtle and elusive ways that are not given conscious, logical formulation.

It is also a peculiarly human phenomenon that a person presents much more information about himself than he is capable of recognizing. At any moment in time each of us reveals to the outside world a huge manifold of cues out of which only a small number are experienced within awareness. Man realizes very little of what is taking place within him. He senses unformed feelings, gropings for words, efforts to put things into rational forms. But he is largely unmindful of the preliminary nonrational states ushering in his later ordered mentation.

Moreover, his most important creative ideas do not always arise in the setting of logical and scientific thinking. On the contrary, they seem to arrive *de novo,* more or less in the form of a hunch, a hunch not founded on consciously understood and prepared data. One's previous thinking, memory processes, and training undoubtedly have to do with the hunch, but nevertheless the hunch, as a variant of thinking, appears in an insular form apparently unconnected with any logical immediate understanding.

Furthermore, the hunch (or the "stochastic" method of thinking, as Linus Pauling has termed it),[1] the dream, the

1] Linus Pauling, "The Stochastic Method and the Structure of Proteins," *American Scientist,* XLIII, No. 2, April, 1955.

an argument for the use of some new techniques in psychotherapy. We shall attempt to provide a valid frame of reference for doing things in the therapeutic interview which have been open to scientific question or have provoked needless anxiety in the therapist.

We shall propose that the therapist does not—and cannot—operate in the therapeutic situation as the unemotional, rational, detached, nonparticipant observer of the present psychoanalytic ideal. Rather, he will always be changing the interaction by virtue of his own problems, prejudices, and perspectives, and the patient will be responding to them. The question then arises: How can the nonrational forms of communication between patient and therapist be put to use to enrich the understanding of the patient's life problems? This view of the analytic process involves a departure from the traditional concept of the patient-therapist relationship and a redefinition of the therapist's role in terms of the inviolable aspects of man's feeling structure.

We hope in presenting our argument to make clear why we have departed rather radically from Freud's position in this specific regard and why we believe that a broader conceptual framework of symbolism for psychoanalysis would advance dream analysis as a therapeutic tool.

Freud's theory of man states basically that there are powerful infantile instinctual forces which have to be gratified, and the neurosis is the compromise which the individual makes when his constitution or the social pressures upon him make it impossible for him to resolve instinctual tensions. The dream, like the symptom, is an avenue which the

extrasensory perception, the insight, and what has been called "the moment of creative illumination and discovery" —all these phenomena are similar in that they are experienced as a unique presentation. They come to a person in a particular symbolic form pregnant with a sense of value, interest, and excitement. The strongly felt hunch puts one in touch with the deeper emotional content of the creative unconscious.

In everyday life the prelogical processes are operative in all interpersonal relationships and form the vast backdrop to every variety of human enterprise and contact. In effect, the most important thing that goes on within man and between man and man is involved with these covert referential processes. A great deal of what we do among one another consists in apprehending nonpropositional emotional responses and reacting to them. Most interpersonal interaction, in fact, goes on in the prelogical mode. We are constantly negating prelogical processes and converting them unwittingly into logical syntactical propositions, with a consequent falsification of security and communication.

One must infer that nonverbal subthreshold "arrangement" is frequently the determining factor in highly significant decisions such as marriage, friendships, and sexual collaboration where unusual or sophisticated nuances are called for. In the negative sense, aversions to collaborations with others achieve their destination in like fashion.

A well-known clinical phenomenon concerns the subtle perceptiveness that homosexuals have in correctly spotting other homosexuals at almost a glance. The cues may be ever so minimal and might be insufficient to alert the unsuspecting; nevertheless they filter through faithfully to those concerned with such matters. Similarly, striking perspicacity in the selection of partners is called for when seemingly unusual sexual activity is sought. In marriage we see, at least in those married people who visit the psychiatrist, the type of mating which exquisitely defines the neurotic needs of the partners. This capacity to pick out the partner is rooted in subthreshold perception and has little to do with the official explanation of the choice made. Persons who have a strong antipathy for various minority groups, and are therefore obsessively concerned with identifying members of such groups, are perhaps more attuned to whatever clues reveal this identification than are persons for whom such a discovery is less important.

Given the pervasiveness of the prelogical thought processes in human experience, it is not surprising that they should play a prominent role in the therapeutic situation. Our interest in this phenomenon grew out of two preliminary investigations into spontaneous responses which one of the authors experienced in relation to the patient (countertransference). In exploring these counter-transference responses, we found that the therapist had identified himself with certain significant figures in the patient's past with minimal prior conscious description of these figures. We were forced to conclude that subthreshold cues "generated" by the patient were unwittingly "received" by the therapist. (We shall discuss this experience in greater detail in Chapter 10.) It is our view that the extent to which such cues can be experienced by the analyst and projected back to the patient probably determines the degree of effective empathy and rapport between them. Freud first pointed out that a transference relationship (the patient's unconscious identification

of the analyst with significant figures in the patient's past) must be established; yet the analyst has to maintain his anonymity—to separate what and where he really is from these past figures—and exploit this therapeutically.

We observed that counter-transference phenomena frequently occurred in the presentational modes such as illogical thoughts, hunches, daydreams, and sleep dreams. These phenomena, when closely attended to, revealed the existence of previously unnoted interactions between the doctor and patient as such and were also representative of other significant interaction on a level ordinarily unperceived by either participant. Thus the analyst's prelogical thoughts could be a bridge to the subthreshold communication existing between the patient and himself.

We have become increasingly aware of the pervasive role played by the prelogical processes in the therapeutic situation. We have also been made aware of the amount of communication that goes on between analyst and patient below the level of awareness. The analytic setting is most fruitfully exploited, we believe, when the analyst pays close attention to the finer nuances of response instead of confining his work to the more explicitly goal-directed therapeutic enterprise. We do not mean to imply that we have rediscovered free association. But we feel that the fuller utilization of the spectrum of referential processes—not only logical, but also prelogical thinking, at threshold and subthreshold levels of awareness, including varying complexities of perceptual and affective experiences—provides the therapist and the patient with more creative areas for investigation.

This book purports to present a logical and practical argument for a new approach to psychotherapy or, more exact-

individual establishes for partial satisfaction of these powerful instinctual needs.

Freud's theory of dream interpretation evolved early in his work on developing a technique for treating hysteria and other psychoneuroses. Like his approach to psychotherapy in general, his approach to dreams was already presaged in his differences with Breuer as seen in the *Studies in Hysteria.* Breuer had emphasized a particular state of consciousness, which he called the hypnoid state, as the etiological agent, while Freud emphasized the neurophysiological quantity of inhibited sexual excitation. This emphasis was to be the cornerstone of his theoretical position from then on.

In Freud's theory the neurophysiologic unit, the nerve cell, is taken as the conceptual model for human behavior. Hence the organism, like the neurone, receives stimulation from internal and external sources. Like the neurone, it must also discharge this electrochemical charge, this quantity of psychic energy, after it accumulates beyond a certain point. Freud used the term *libido* to designate this qualitatively distinct kind of energy that accumulates from specific chemical processes that are unknown. The release of the libido is constitutionally structured—either channeled within the soma or discharged through the erotogenic zones. Its damming up in the central nervous system is biologically unsatisfactory and only serves to give hallucinatory intensity to wish-images.

Freud's theory of dreams addressed itself also to man's need for restful sleep, as well as to his need to deal with sexual excitation. Thus he postulated that the dream served as the guardian of sleep. This sleep-preserving function of

7

the dream has been traditionally demonstrated in dream material, particularly that of children, where the dreamer hallucinatorily satisfies needs like hunger, thirst, elimination, and obligations such as being dressed to go to school or to work.

However, the most striking aspect of his theory of dreams dealt with the problem of libidinal excitation. The tendency to hallucinatory wish fulfillment characterized for Freud the earliest mental processes of human life, which continued to operate unconsciously in later life. He called this type of process primary process. Early in life the biological frustration, i.e., the painful accumulation of excitation within the central nervous system, provokes a modification of the mental apparatus for insuring more adequate satisfaction by testing the reality of the outer world. He called this modification the ego, and the type of processes governed by reality testing he called secondary process. The primary-process type of thinking is repressed by the ego but tends to emerge whenever the ego is weakened by toxic states, fatigue, serious mental illness, or sleep.

This is seen in the peculiar qualities of dreams. Dreams are produced, according to Freud, by infantile sexual excitations pressing for discharge which have been activated by some extraneous noises or sensations during sleep or by conflicts, doubts, and tensions of the preceding day or two. The dream is a compromise formation resolving the conflict between these wish-impulses that might arouse wakefulness and the old infantile sexual wish to return to the womb, i.e., to sleep. The preconscious ego of the dreamer thus allows a partial satisfaction in hallucinatory wish-fulfillment, the dream; but it must be disguised so that the conscious ego of the dreamer will not be aroused into wakefulness. The unconscious intrapsychic processes that transform the wish-impulses are called dream work. The completed dream as it is remembered and reported by the conscious ego is called the manifest dream or manifest content of the dream, and the wish-impulses disguised in this manifest content comprise the latent content of the dream, or latent dream thoughts.

Despite Freud's avowed attempt in *The Interpretation of Dreams* to establish a separate domain for dream interpretation, he discovered that he was unable to separate his theory of dreams from his conceptualization of psychopathology in general. In this book, he likened symptom formation to the manifest content of dreams, and the repressed memories and libidinal drives to the latent content. He described certain psychic phenomena equally applicable to dream work and to symptom formation, which he called laws of the unconscious. The three most prominent were the laws of condensation, displacement, and reversal. Condensation is the process whereby a multitude of diverse latent thoughts are condensed into a single element of the manifest content. Displacement consists of dream work that permits a trivial element of the manifest content to acquire great psychic intensity or, vice versa, camouflages the powerful significance of a particular psychic element by divesting it of most if not all of its psychic intensity. Reversal, or turning a thing into its opposite, Freud said, is most favored by the dream work. This means that "high" in the manifest content can refer to "low" in the latent content, "short" means "long," and "black" can mean "white" and so on.

The meaning of a dream, according to Freud, is its latent

content, which can only be arrived at by following the associations of the dreamer and understanding the laws and nature of the unconscious. As he had originally analyzed neurotic symptoms by tracing associations back, layer by layer, so he analyzed manifest dreams, beginning first with associations to the words or fragments of the dream, noting the inconsistencies in the dream, the hesitations that appear in reporting the dream, and the emotionally charged elements in the dream. He made similar investigations into what he called the psychopathology of everyday life—slips of the tongue, absent-mindedness, and unwitting puns—finding here, too, repressed infantile sexuality, unconscious self-reproaches, and so on. Freud maintained his belief in the exclusiveness of the libido to the end. In 1940 he wrote, "The symptoms of neurosis are exclusively, it might be said, either a substitute satisfaction of some sexual impulse or measures to prevent such a satisfaction, and are as a rule compromises between the two." [2]

Freud was fully aware of the difficulties that dream reporting presents, namely, the limited capacity to recall the manifest dream and also the inherent human failing that provides the report with conceptual and verbal props to lend it a discursive form consistent with the forms of everyday common-sense communication. Language ordinarily implies an organized, coherent, meaningful set of statements which can communicate with the foreseeable expectation of the other person. Dream experiences very frequently violate the very conditions for which linguistic communication is designed because of their absurdities, contradictions, space-time dis-

2] Sigmund Freud, *An Outline of Psychoanalysis* (New York: Norton, 1949), p. 85.

orientations, and illogicalities. Despite these serious limitations in dream reporting, Freud regarded the dream as an unswerving path to the understanding of man.

These limitations in dream reporting provoked certain serious scholars to critical thinking and led them to devise experimental methods to meet the emerging challenges presented by dream phenomena. It may be of interest to sketch briefly some of the early experimental work in which hypnotic techniques were used to test the validity of various concepts formulated by Freud, such as the concepts of wish-fulfillment, day residue, censorship, and sexual symbolism.[3] Although these pioneer efforts reveal a curious failure to appreciate the complexity of symbolization in man, they do represent the historical offshoot of Freud's studies on dreams as well as serious attempts to advance our understanding of symbolic processes.

The works of Schroetter, Roffenstein, and Nachmansohn are most frequently cited in this connection.[4] Schroetter's

3] With respect to the possibility of controversy concerning the similarity or differences between the hypnotically induced dream and the normal dream, we offer the following suggestions. As we see it, the attempt to distinguish nuances between the hypnotically induced dream and the conventional night dream seems to be based on the assumption of different kinds of sleep. In other words, the anticipated distinction is rooted in two tacit assumptions: (1) that the state of induced sleep is different from normal sleep and therefore has a modifying effect on the dream and (2) that the specialized influence of the hypnotist-subject relationship is basically different from the usual nonhypnotic personal relationship. The nature of the subject's relationship to the significant people, including the hypnotist, in the experimental situation seems to organize the particular structure and content of the dream. Whatever is available interpersonally to any particular individual within the spectrum of his interpersonal experience can appear in some form in the dream.

4] See David Rapaport, *Organization and Pathology of Thought* (New York: Columbia University Press, 1951), pp. 249-287.

experiments were focused on establishing the effects of suggestion on the form and content of the dream. Experiments were also performed to illustrate the effect of clang association. In the first of his experiments Schroetter put subjects into deep hypnosis, allegedly characterized by unconsciousness followed by amnesia; during this hypnotic state he gave them suggestions to dream. Four to five minutes later the subjects would spontaneously begin to dream. They indicated the beginning and the end of the dream by signs, according to his instructions; thus the duration of the dream could be exactly measured. On awakening, they reported their dreams.

In another series of experiments by Schroetter, the patients were to dream during the night following the suggestion and to write down their dreams on awakening. The findings revealed that elements of the hypnotic suggestions were woven into the character make-up of the subject in the dream and into the interactions of the dreamer with various dream personalities, including the hypnotist. Some of the manifest content appeared in undisguised form, while some appeared in either the symbolic form or what has been called indirect representation. Indirect representation and symbolization in the dream are presumed to be different processes, despite the empirical fact that the distinctions may be difficult if not impossible to agree on with reference to a specific item. Symbolization refers primarily to the expression of repressed, unconscious material; indirect representation refers more to disguised, preconscious material. The existence of wish fulfillment motifs, as conceived of by Freud, was clearly confirmed by Schroetter's work.

The difficulty with accrediting this type of research rests on the scientific method in use. For example, although

Schroetter's findings might easily be valid, the lack of control techniques precludes accepting them as firmly conclusive.

These experiments demonstrated that the dreamer can incorporate in his dream material from the external world which in and of itself contains no rational construction and can then convert this material into a dream story which approximates a rational sequential anecdote. Freud himself had called attention to this capacity in man to fashion a pictorial blend, many of whose brush strokes contain pigments of the day's residue. This phenomenon has been referred to as the regard for intelligibility, rooted in the awakening consciousness and oriented toward intelligible synthesis of the dream elements. (Essentially the same type of experimentation in reference to the psychopathology of everyday life was carried out by Erickson utilizing hypnotic techniques. He too was able to demonstrate the subjects' creative utilization of suggested fragments along with the incidental percepts in the experimental setting.)

Roffenstein's work was intended to test the validity of the Freudian symbolic interpretation of dreams. He gave subjects suggestions, under hypnosis, to dream of sexual activities, with the command for post-hypnotic amnesia. The post-hypnotic dreams revealed symbolically the sexual activities suggested, without direct expression of sexuality in the manifest content. His findings are alleged to have confirmed Freud's discovery of sexual symbols. The material of the dream produced experimentally under hypnotic suggestion contained symbolic elements but also elements of the suggestion itself in undisguised form.

Nachmansohn extended the early researches by demonstrating the sleep-protective function of the dream and the operation of censorship and sexual symbolism in dreams. In the first of his experiments he gave his subject the hypnotic suggestion that if the headache she had been having should return, she should dream about it without awakening. The dream then served to protect her sleep.

Nachmansohn further tested the role of censorship in restricting the symbolization used in waking thought and in directing the disguises assumed in the symbols of the dream. He showed that hypnotically induced situations in waking life and in sleep can be carried through provided that the defensive requirements of the subject's personality are not challenged. In addition to confirming the validation of psychoanalytic theory established by the earlier experiments of Schroetter and Roffenstein, he anticipated later thinking in suggesting the powerful creativity inherent in the dream.

Although the experiments cited established the fact that some symbols are used preferentially, indicating universality of meaning, it is the form, not the content, of the symbol that is the vehicle of representation. A snake or a church spire can be symbols of the phallus by virtue of their elongated form, not their intrinsic meaning. As has been pointed out by students of language and metaphor, when a person wants to describe or express something for which he does not have the immediate conventional vocabulary, he will use the simplest correlated form that comes to mind—it is simple to use an elongated object to represent an elongated object.

Why some parts of the dream appear undisguised, other parts in indirect representation, and yet others in symbolic form has been a puzzling question to students of the organization and pathology of thought. It is our impression that the attempt to classify specific items of mental activity in line with specified modes of symbolization, as if certain thoughts and feelings must fall precisely into a specified slot, creates something of a pseudo-problem. We do not believe that one can anticipate rigorously how significantly distressing any particular emotional item will be for any one individual. We agree in general that the more threatening items will undergo the greatest degree of disguise (dissociation), but this is essentially a private datum which cannot be anticipated precisely for any specific person. Therefore one must recognize that an item which might apparently be highly charged for the hypnotist or analyst need not necessarily have equally distressing meaning for the subject or patient. Thus the patient might surprise the therapist by producing undisguised material simply because he is not threatened, and not because he is insensitive or refractory.

One of the glaring difficulties in carrying out psychoanalytic research comes from the discovery of man's all-pervasive infantile tendencies toward magical wish fulfillment. Anticipation of the effects of these tendencies has blocked extensive psychoanalytic research. The analyst is only too keenly aware of the temptation to see his wishes fulfilled, and therefore can never feel certain that his studies of other human beings may not be essentially subjective. If the experiments confirm his hypothesis, he is harassed by the fear that his subjects were compliant; if they fail to confirm his hypothesis, he cannot be sure that his human subjects did not have a "need" to frustrate him.

The only hope to transcend this dilemma lies in allowing oneself to become a part of the very experiment one has strenuously sought to isolate oneself from. The dangers of subjectivity are not resolved by being outside the experimental field. The great human paradox is that true separateness can only exist in true fusion and vice versa. The approximation to objective truth is thus accomplished through the incorporation of all interactional data.

Thus in attempting to appraise the early climate of psychoanalytic inquiry and research methods, one is struck today by the understandable paucity of issues considered significant for fruitful discovery. For example, the problem of understanding what goes on between patient and doctor is far richer and far more intricate than who submits to whom, or who dominates whom. The reductive implications of such a theory violate the nature and dignity of man's existence.

Despite the impressive capacity to correlate different aspects of man's nature within a unified theoretical system, this very oversimplification conduces to a neglect of many of the phenomenological aspects of man which properly define his uniqueness. A great deal more is transpiring in the field of man's human existence than Freud considered worthy of attention. Very complex selective processes go on in man which help to define what is permissible and significant in awareness from what would be bewildering, misleading, or frightening. It is important for an appropriate psychologic theory to recognize the patterning and distribution of symbolic processes operating throughout the range of awareness and beyond into the inferential range of unawareness.

Any study of the symbolic process in man is deeply complex because of the vast confluence of essentially uncapturable nonverbal processes further complicated by servomechanisms which are out of conscious control. The virtuoso on the violin and the jet pilot, for example, are constantly reacting to myriads of percepts, too amazingly complicated to be given verbal formulation. In our development of dream theory we attempt to utilize a broader frame of reference for the interpretation of dreams than Freud advocated, applying the concept of symbolism to the continuity of conscious and unconscious mental activity.

In recent years reconsideration of the classical picture concerning symbols has led several investigators [5] to question the existence of fixity, universality, transition states between true symbolism and indirect representation, and to recognize the dangers of reification with respect to symbol formation.

Kubie describes the symbolic process as a function involving contact with the inner world and the outer world.[6] This implies, if followed to its legitimate conclusion, that the boundaries of man dynamically extend beyond the surface of his integument. This is no mere figure of speech; it means that the contactual process with other people inheres in man's very existence. The dream, perhaps better than any other symbolic performance in man, bridges the gap between the inner and outer world.

The exclusive emphasis which Freud placed upon motivational dynamics has to some extent invaded the broader use-

5] Emilio Rodriqué, "Notes on Symbolism," *Intern. J. of Psychol.*, XXXVII, 137–157.

6] Lawrence S. Kubie, *J. of Am. Psychoan. Assn.*, I (1953), 59. Rycroft, in a recent paper, follows Kubie and others in rejecting the distinction made by Freud and Jones between different kinds of symbolism. He takes a wider view of symbolism, applying it as we do to the continuity of conscious and unconscious mental activity. *See* Rycroft, "Symbolism and the Primary and Secondary Process," *Internat. J. of Psychol.*, XXXVII, 137–146.

fulness of psychoanalytic therapy and, we believe, has interfered with an appreciation of the many-sidedness of man's
living. As a result, although the rules laid down for dream
interpretation are not always slavishly followed, therapists
tend to avoid using spontaneity when in reality one of the
basic purposes of analysis is to bring out the patient's spontaneity. The more perceptive patient might recognize that
much pandering to the scientific approach to dreams, where
only what the patient says is considered valuable entree to
his unconscious, is oversimplification and an expression of
fear of the therapist's engagement with the patient.

Both philosophically and practically it is essential to utilize
the novelty that resides in the dream. Dreams analyzed at an
earlier period in the therapeutic situation often come up for
discussion again weeks and months later. It is obvious that
if one relies upon a standardized fixed interpretation of the
dream, any future discussion becomes logically redundant,
and further spontaneous thought and feeling are not provoked. One cannot deny that the same dream heard months
or even years later often evokes fresh reactions. These new
reactions do not mean that the original reactions or responses to the dream were necessarily incorrect, but that
new facets of response have occurred both in the patient and
in the analyst and that these new responses are evidence of
the constant novelty and openness of the therapeutic situation. An unalterable, stable response over long periods to the
same dream suggests blocking. Obviously much new has occurred in the patient's life—or at least let us hope that it
has—therefore the symbols of the dream should have new
meanings for patient and therapist. A fixity of set in this

area must transmit itself to other domains of the therapeutic work. We have observed during supervisory work as well as in continuous case seminars that a re-examination of certain dream material, after varying periods of time and with additional data about the patient, provides the observer with further communicative ideas concerning the patient, thereby bringing together many seemingly loose ends in the analytic enterprise.

The dream has occupied an impressive role in the vast prelogical manifold that exists in man's nature. It has received much more attention because it is a dramatic and unusual presentation. However, our book deals also with other prelogical developments which only in recent years have acquired sufficient status to permit of scientific investigation.[7]

In making these statements, we are not repudiating what has been earned by Freud's wisdom, nor are we urging that the pendulum must now swing in the opposite direction. Yet one cannot approach any type of original investigation, of which every psychoanalytic enterprise is a good illustration, without recognizing that every hour must be regarded as a fresh experience. It must be approached in the spirit of true scientific inquiry; and an unimaginative adherence to rules that can actually serve no useful purpose will never

7] Lawrence S. Kubie in his book *Neurotic Distortion of the Creative Process* (Porter Lectures, Series 22. Lawrence: University of Kansas Press, 1958) has presented views concerning symbolizing processes which are essentially in agreement with our own. He, however, has definitely organized his conceptualization of the unconscious, preconscious, and conscious systems. In his formulation, the preconscious system is the essential agent of creativity. This is an extremely provocative thesis. Challenging though it is, one is confronted with the danger of reification.

lead to the heart of the mystery. The chain of process no longer has to be rooted so deeply in direct observation and measurement. Thus, we can dare to adventure into areas of human operation which defy the need for simple, observable fact with the hope of rich discovery derived from creative imagination.

2

Language, Symbols, & Scientific Method

Aᴌᴛʜᴏᴜɢʜ a great deal of the present thinking in psychoanalysis is oriented in the direction of the physical sciences, there is reason to question whether scientific methodology provides an adequate approach to the psychological study of man when psychoanalysis is examined in the light of its own principles and goals. The symbolic theories in science are based on abstractive systems of thinking that are highly pertinent to the study of the physical world. But elements enter the human situation which play no significant role in the physical world. The fact of these differences seems to call for a methodology rooted in different conceptual and symbolic foundations from those of the physical sciences.

Certainly traditional scientific methods have not been

strikingly fruitful as an approach to the psychological under-standing of man. Emotional reactions, attitudes, systems of values, creative trends, patterns of interaction, inhibitions—to mention only a few of the phenomena met with in man—have not been productively studied so far. Furthermore, it is extremely doubtful that data on such phenomena could be organized for analysis by even the most elaborate elec-tronic devices. A scientific study of meaning in art, literature, and all forms of human enterprise clearly requires a different approach.

These comments are not made with the intention of dis-crediting scientific method or of hinting at a sensational solu-tion. They are intended only to suggest that our basic ap-proach to the study of man needs to be re-examined. Are we overlooking certain possibilities of expanding the total grasp of the human situation?

The conventional grammar of logic employed in the scien-tific study of the physical world is applicable with great rigor to problems that can be examined in terms of their literal content. But the study of emotional problems seems to call for a somewhat different mode of exploration.

In the modern history of ideas, the distinction is made between the types of questions that have meaning within the framework of knowledge called logical conception and those which fall outside this framework into the realm of meta-physical speculation. The study of symbolic logic shows that there is, inherent in language usage, a set of properties which permit certain ideas to be expressed but will be inadequate to express certain other ideas. Thus Carnap defines the limits of scientific inquiry as follows:

> *I can ask whatever language will express; I can know whatever experiment will answer. A proposition which could not, under any . . . conditions, be verified or refuted, is a pseudoproposition, it has no literal meaning. It does not belong to the framework of knowledge that we call logical conception; it is not true or false, but* unthinkable, *for it falls outside the order of symbolism.*[1]

The rather large amount of our talk and our thinking that defies the canons of literal meaning—those metaphysical propositions that can neither be affirmed nor denied, although they clearly and continuously interest man—Carnap calls "analogous to laughing in that they have only an expressive function, no representative function."[2]

Similarly, Bertrand Russell says,

> *I do not deny the importance or value, within its own sphere, of the kind of philosophy which is inspired by ethical notions. The ethical work of Spinoza, for instance, appears to me of the very highest significance, but what is valuable in such a work is not any metaphysical theory as to the nature of the world to which it may give rise, nor indeed anything that can be proved or disproved by argument. What is valuable is the indication of some new way of feeling toward life and the world, some way of feeling by which our own existence can acquire more of the characteristics which we most deeply desire.*[3]

1] Susanne K. Langer, *Philosophy in a New Key* (New York: Mentor, 1958), p. 78.
2] Rudolf Carnap, *Philosophy and Logical Syntax* (London: Routledge, 1935), p. 28.
3] Bertrand Russell, "Scientific Method and Philosophy," in *Mysticism and Logic* (New York: W. W. Norton, 1918), p. 109.

The formal logic of symbols assumes that "the knowable is a clearly defined field, governed by the requirements of discursive projectability. Outside this domain is the inexpressible realm of feeling, of formless desires and satisfactions, immediate experience, forever incognito and incommunicado." [4] An expert in symbolic logic would accuse a philosopher who looks in that direction of being a mystic.

"So long as we admit only discursive symbolism as a bearer of ideas, 'thought' in this restricted sense must be regarded as our only intellectual activity. It begins and ends with language; without the elements, at least, of scientific grammar, conception must be impossible." [5]

But "there is an unexplored possibility of genuine semantic beyond the limits of discursive language." [6] We have to recognize that the field of semantics is actually wider than that of language, as philosophers such as Schopenhauer, Dewey, Cassirer, and Whitehead have discovered. The failure to explore such a semantic can be attributed to the fundamental assumption of current epistemology that *"language is the only means of articulating thought."* [7] "Our confidence in language," Bertrand Russell comments, "is due to the fact that it . . . shares the structure of the physical world, and therefore can express that structure. But if there be a world which is not physical, or not in space-time, it may have a structure which we can never hope to express or to know." [8]

To Russell's idea, Susanne Langer replies:

> . . . *in this physical, space-time world of our experience there are things which do not fit the grammatical scheme*

4] Langer, *op. cit.,* pp. 80–81.
5] *Ibid.,* p. 82.   6] *Ibid.,* p. 81.   7] *Ibid.*
8] Bertrand Russell, *Philosophy* (New York: W. W. Norton, 1927), p. 265.

of expression. But they are not necessarily blind, inconceivable, mystical affairs; they are simply matters which require to be conceived through some symbolistic schema other than discursive language. . . . Language is by no means our only articulate product. Our merest sense-experience is a process of formulation. . . . A tendency to organize the sensory field into groups and patterns of sense-data, to perceive forms rather than a flux of light-impressions, seems to be inherent in our receptor apparatus just as much as in the higher nervous centers with which we do arithmetic and logic. But this unconscious appreciation of forms is the primitive root of all abstraction, which in turn is the keynote of rationality.[9]

Mental life is a situation in which we often regard repeated experiences as analogous occurrences. We see the familiarities in situations primarily because we abstract from our sense data and organize situations so that we have, constructed out of sensory experience, certain formalized conceptions of a situation as a whole. Thus sense data as such would be useless to a mind whose activity is thoroughly a symbolic process. There must be some way of dealing with the forms to which the individual is exposed; and, of course, with this notion one can infer that the sensory receptacles are already active before material reaches the mind and the abstractive process is put into motion. "A mind that works primarily with meanings must have organs that supply it primarily with forms." [10] Thus the mind is operative on its own level, but still the impingement of outside experience on the sensory organs must already consist in a certain kind of mentation. Seeing is "not a passive process, by which meaningless impressions are stored up for the use of an organizing

9] Langer, *op. cit.*, pp. 82–83.   10] *Ibid.*, p. 84.

mind, which construes forms out of these amorphous data to suit its own purposes. 'Seeing' is itself a process of formulation; our understanding of the visible world begins in the eye." [11] This approach, attributed to the school of Wertheimer, Köhler, and Koffka, has very far-reaching philosophical consequences, for it indicates in a sense that a kind of rationality operates in a setting which is usually regarded as prerational. Thus there is the possibility of symbolic material operative "at a level where symbolic activity has certainly never been looked for by any epistemologist. The eye and the ear make their own abstractions, and consequently dictate their own peculiar forms of conception." [12]

This would mean that there is no such thing as *the* form of the world. "Physics is one pattern which may be found in it, and 'appearance,' or the pattern of *things* with their qualities and characters, is another. One construction may indeed preclude the other; but to maintain that the consistency and universality of the one brands the other as *false* is a mistake." [13]

Furthermore, the facts of physical analysis do not rest on the final establishment of irreducible qualities, do not refute that there are red, blue, and green things, wet or oily substances, fragrant and ill-smelling flowers, shiny and dull surfaces. "These concepts . . . are not approximations to 'physical' notions at all. Physical concepts owe their origin and development to the application of *mathematics* to the world of 'things,' and mathematics never . . . dealt with qualities of objects. It measured their proportions, but never treated its concepts . . . as qualities of which *so-and-so much* could become an ingredient of certain objects. . . . To suppose that

11] *Ibid.*   12] *Ibid.*, p. 85.   13] *Ibid.*

the 'material mode' is a primitive and groping attempt at physical conception is a fatal error in epistemology, because it cuts off all interest in the developments of which sensuous conception is capable, and the intellectual uses to which it might be put." [14]

L. A. Reid, in his *Knowledge and Truth,* "admits the facts of non-propositional conception in a way that invites rather than precludes logical analysis." Visual forms such as lines, colors, and proportions are just as capable of articulation as words, but the laws that govern this sort of articulation are different from the laws of syntax that govern language. Of course,

> *the most radical difference is that* visual forms are not discursive. *They do not present their constituents successively, but simultaneously, so the relations determining a visual structure are grasped in one act of vision. Their complexity, consequently, is not limited, as the complexity of discourse is limited, by what the mind can retain from the beginning of an apperceptive act to the end of it. . . . An idea that contains too many minute yet closely related parts, too many relations within relations, cannot be "projected" into discursive form; it is too subtle for speech. A language-bound theory of mind, therefore, rules it out of the domain of understanding and the sphere of knowledge.*[15]

This material brings us to certain theoretical ideas concerning dream analysis. Dreams, as we know, are usually presented in the form of visual imagery. Therefore, in order to communicate a dream to a listener, one has to translate its visual imagery into a language which is meaningful to the listener. Thus one is immediately confronted with something extraordinarily difficult because of the kaleidoscopic

14] *Ibid.*   15] *Ibid.,* p. 86.

piling up of so many different meanings. Wherever communication involves much more than language can adequately express, there is high probability of serious gaps, misunderstanding, improper inference, and so on. The psychotherapeutic session can be exquisitely handicapped by just such conditions. The communication of dream material perhaps most strikingly illustrates the weakness of the tool of language. A large part of man's experience is totally nonpropositional in quality.

How have the leading theorists in psychoanalysis dealt with this impasse? Some have skillfully avoided the dread whirlpools of boundless subjective speculation; others have plunged in fearlessly, attempting to capture a theme here and there, unmindful of the stringent restrictions of scientific method; still others have taken a middle path, somewhat eclectically searching for what may best aid in the patient's cure.

Most theoreticians have been averse to an epistemology other than positivism.

In contrast, although capable of utilizing the more powerful aspects of Freud's contributions, Fromm nevertheless recognizes the essentially nonpropositional matrix of man's life. Not restricted to seeing man in simple biochemical or physiological terms, he approaches the study of man by posing profound questions concerning man's existence. He reflects that man is in a great assortment of ways attempting to answer the question of his existence; yet he recognizes that man's solution to this existence is essentially an unconsciously designed process. He takes the position that we have to address ourselves to what are the problems of man, availing ourselves of a symbolic formulation which

comes closest to identifying the issues at hand. Some theoreticians have criticized Fromm on the grounds that he
deals with ethics and values—areas uncongenial to the scientific method. They view his thinking as religious and mystical, leading away from profitable scientific growth. This
view, we believe, is a mistaken one. It repudiates an essential
ingredient of human interaction and also oversimplifies its
complexity by deleting that which cannot be comfortably
assimilated. Fromm broadened the scope of dream interpretation by his recognition that, through immediate contact,
the many-sided quality of man's nature is revealed by his
dreams.[16] This breadth seems in part to derive from his being
unencumbered by traditional scientific attitudes.

The literature shows that many analysts are inclined to
interpret the dream in a metaphorical sense. Freud himself,
in *The Interpretation of Dreams,* uses the method of metaphoric interpretation. Metaphoric interpretation comes closest
to artistic interpretation. That is, one does not analyze the
dream by breaking it down into very simple elements, any
more than one interprets a poem in terms of its component
words and phrases. Rather, the dream, like the poem, excites
the listener to a certain type of emotional experience which
has a meaning of its own. Sometimes this emotional experience can be verbalized and sometimes it cannot. If it can
be verbalized, of course, the treatment of the dream experience approximates propositional form; its further logical
inferences can be derived. In actual practice the therapist
asks for free associations either because the dream is not sufficiently self-evident to him or because he feels that by further
free association it will become more meaningful to him even

16] Erich Fromm, *The Forgotten Language* (New York: Rinehart, 1951).

though it may continue to remain rather meaningless to the patient.

The danger is that the analyst will interpret the material of free association to fit his own theory and be unmindful of the patient's problem. The metaphorical interpretation is less vulnerable to this danger because it deals much more with simply formulating the presentational experience into communicable form, thus respecting the individuality of the patient's picture. This encouragement of metaphorical exposition stimulates a variety of pictures of the self in action, leading to flexibility of meaning and the avoidance of premature concretization. An oversimplified adherence to a theoretical end-goal interferes with maintaining the novelty of creative exploration. For scientific interchange, of course, the extent to which communication by the patient can be formulated in abstractive form determines the degree to which it can be utilized by other therapists. Nondiscursive symbols cannot be defined in terms of others as discursive symbols can. But the genuine virtues of scientific rigor can easily be misapplied in the early phase of a scientific venture.

The symbolic forms of man's thought have not come suddenly into being but have emerged as a continuous development through the history of his language and culture; and for each individual they have evolved through his own particular life history. Human intelligence begins with the prime mental activity, conception. The process of conception always culminates in symbolic expression, for a conception is fixed and held only when it has been embodied in its symbol. So the study of symbolic forms offers a key to the forms of human conception.

The origin of symbolic forms—verbal, religious, artistic, mathematical, or whatever modes of expression there may be —is the odyssey of the mind. The two oldest of these modes seem to be language and myth. Both are of prehistoric birth, so it is impossible to fix the age of either of them; but there are many reasons for regarding them as twin creatures. The intuitions about nature and man reflected in the oldest verbal roots and the processes by which language probably originated are the same intuitions and the same processes as those expressed in the development of myths. They do not follow the canons of discursive logic, the forms of reason which underlie both common sense and logic. Reason is not man's primitive endowment but his achievement. Logic springs from language when language has reached maturity. Myth never breaks out of the magic circle of primitive thinking with its figurative mode of expression. It reaches religious and poetic heights, but the gulf between its conceptions and those of science never narrows. But language, born in that same magic circle, has the power to break its bonds. Language takes us from the myth-making phase of human mentality to the phase of logical thought and factual conception.

Theories of knowledge have in general treated the final achievement as man's natural and primitive way of thinking, and facts as his earliest stock in trade. As a result, most of man's actual ideas, the fruits of his cultural and spiritual background, have had to be discounted as error, caprice, or emotional indulgence because they do not fit into this conceptual framework. A philosophy of symbolic form, however, is based on the recognition that the philosophy of mind involves much more than a theory of knowledge: it involves the theory of prelogical conception and expression and their final culmination in reason, factual knowledge, and art.

Dreams, like language and myths, are part of man's inherent background and inherent potential, and the dreaming process has much of the prelogical quality that characterizes the processes of mind operative in the myth and in the origins of language. Language has the capacity to develop syntactical structure which prepares its use for rigorous scientific formulation. The myth, on the other hand, is never logical in the sense of scientific logic, although it has a logic of its own. Cassirer says of the mythical consciousness: "Above all, it lacks any fixed dividing line between mere representation and real perception, between wish and fulfillment, between image and thing." This could also be a description of the dream consciousness. In his sleep the human being employs the prehistorical, prelogical thought processes of the primitive myth-maker. An appreciation of dreams from this broader philosophical and philological point of view is not only important in considering a theory of dreams or dream interpretation, but also in grasping the nature and significance of presentational experience in general.

3

The Creative Function
of the Image

A GLANCE at the role that the image-making faculty has played in man's cultural history and the creative experience of man strengthens the impression based upon clinical observation that there is a fallacy in identifying the prelogical processes with infancy, a chronological condition. Prelogical thinking is part of the basic endowment of man throughout life which operates continuously. This type of thinking is not something which existed in infancy and is dragged inertly along through later life, contaminating adult experience. It is out of the well-springs of prelogical thinking that ordered logical thinking can finally emerge. Thus dream material relating to primitive thought and feeling can and often does relate to the present and even to the foreseeable future, and not necessarily to infancy.

Man's intuitive subjective insight into the truth about himself and his world has always preceded his power to give objective logical formulation to this truth. Thus myth, which presents the idea as image, is always a forerunner of science, as poetry is of prose. Language itself has its origins in man's inherent tendency to give form and appearance to his feelings and thoughts in metaphor. In the creative activity of individual man, as in the creative activity of the race, the image plays an equally significant role. Poets and artists throughout the ages have told of the image that "comes" as a step in the creative experience, and many discoveries of far-reaching consequence in science have come as a brilliant flash of intuitive insight, rather than as a logical deduction from observable fact.

Cassirer, in his study of the mythical consciousness of man, shows how the image has functioned in the historical development of knowledge:

> The mythical world is concrete, not because it has to do with sensuous, objective contents, not because it excludes and repels all merely abstract factors—all that is merely signification and sign; it is concrete because in it the two factors, thing and signification, are undifferentiated, because they merge, flow together, concresce in an immediate unity. . . . This concrescence of name and thing in the linguistic consciousness of primitives and children might be illustrated by a number of striking examples. (We need only think of the various forms of name tabus.) But as language develops, a differentiation becomes sharper and more constant. . . . Distinct from all merely physical existence and all physical efficacy the word emerges in its own specificity, in its purely ideal, significatory function. And art leads us to still another stage of detachment. . . . Here for the first time the image world acquires a purely immanent validity and truth. It does not aim at something else or refer to something else; it simply "is" and consists in itself.

The Creative Function of the Image

From the sphere of efficacy to which the mythical conscious-ness clings and the sphere of signification in which the lin-guistic sign perseveres we are transposed into a sphere where, as it were, only the pure reality, only the intrinsic and inherent essence, of the image is apprehended as such. Thus for the first time the world of the image becomes a self-contained cosmos with its own center of gravity. . . . Measured by empirical, realistic criteria, the aesthetic world becomes a world of ap-pearance; but in severing its bonds with immediate reality, with material existence and efficacy which constitute the world of magic and myth, it embodies a new step toward the truth.[1]

The genuine symbol is the phenomenal form of under-lying ideas. It is the stringent psychological laws governing this form that lend symbols their imperative character. Dreams and neurotic symptoms, like the cosmogonic myths of the ancients, are pictorial images determined by inner necessity and not by arbitrary agreement. But although the symbol is the necessary form of appearance of a group of ideas under given conditions, it cannot be cognized as a mere symbol by the one in whose mind it comes into exist-ence. If it could be so cognized, and one could state that idea A is merely an image or a symbol of idea B, the idea under-lying the symbol could appear to the mind's eye in form B also. If, however, we consider that for each given stage of mental development and each given state of mind there is only one possible form of manifestation of an idea, then form B cannot as yet be clearly in consciousness when it is form A that corresponds to that stage of development or that state of mind. Modern ethnological and linguistic re-

1] E. Cassirer, *Philosophy of Symbolic Form* (New Haven: Yale University Press, 1955), vol. 2, pp. 25, 36.

search, in fact, contends that myths are not merely metaphorical expressions, allegory-like pictures deliberately invented by primitive people, but rather are the only possible expression of the conception of nature, given the state of mental development at the time. A people who speak in metaphors do not experience what they say as metaphors; the symbols they use are regarded not as symbols, but as realities.

To the dreamer too his dream images appear not as mere symbols but rather as the real relation of things. And the compulsion-neurotic has no notion, unless apprized, that his obsessive ideas and compulsive actions are mere symbols, circumscriptions of something underlying them, substitute formations for ideas and feelings that can present themselves to him only in such forms. No one whose apperception is symbolic can at the time be clearly aware of that fact or of the extent of his symbolic activity.

The kind of symbolic practices that one is engaged in would be a function, on the one hand, of the intellectual and emotional development of the individual, his maturation. On the other hand, it would also be a function of his particular state of consciousness at the time—whether he is awake or asleep and the extent to which he is alert or cloudy or whatever. Thus in the state of consciousness connected with intoxication or fever or drug influence, for example, one would expect some modification of the type of symbolic phenomena as compared with those manifested in the normal waking states. However, some confusion exists because symbolizing processes operative in one state of consciousness or maturation may unexpectedly emerge in an "inappropriate" stage of consciousness and maturation; for example, the person in a fugue state, the sleepwalker, and so on. It means that general laws operate in symbolism, and the laws usually respect certain modifications connected with states of consciousness and also with stages of maturation.

In relation to this, it is important to recognize how urgency and interest affect consciousness. Values and interests may be approached hierarchically from either the criterion of urgency or that of quality. Extreme urgency characterizes a situation in which life itself is at stake and all one's energies are intensely used in preserving life in the face of the threats to it. This type of urgent interest is demonstrated in relation to food in a situation of starvation, to water in a situation of severe thirst, and to companionship in a situation of desperate loneliness. There may also be the same type of urgent interest in a mediating other-person, as when the infant cries desperately for its mother, using all its energy most intensely to make its cry heard.

Other types of urgent interest occur in situations where, although life itself is not necessarily threatened, timing is so crucial that lack of response to timing may be disastrous. All these situations have certain qualities in common: extreme urgency is a now-and-forever, later-is-never, all-or-nothing, yes-or-no type of process. There is a gradient, however, from most extreme urgency over significant time intervals to the opposite extreme of indefinite postponement and permanent inattention. The awareness that is determined by urgency is related more to the temporal circumstances than to the nature of the object or activity itself. The form of the psychological set involved differs, depending upon whether it arises predominantly out of the quality of a situation or out of crucial timing.

Disease, injury to the brain, drugs, and alcohol have certain consequences in common; all these conditions change a person's interaction with the outside world. The atttitude taken toward such a person is that he must be given more leeway in this interaction and treated more permissively. He is also not expected to be as expert in his performance as persons not similarly affected. In other words, value systems are modified under these conditions. The person himself believes that he can do things with a little more abandon. He is able to express affects such as aggression, affection, laughter, criticism, and so on with less censoring of his feelings in these matters; and the outside world, although perhaps inconvenienced and annoyed by his conduct, does not hold him as responsible.

Now whether there has really been a change is seriously open to question. Quite possibly the drugs or alcohol or brain injury has simply allowed the person's values to show more prominently. It is as if one had thrown a light on a statue from a new angle, sharpening aspects which had previously been obscured by shadows; the statue now appears different, but it is still the same statue. There is a shift of balances and credits in a somewhat stable system which is virtually a change rather than actually a change. The actual change is in the ability to make discriminations, especially in terms of foreseeing what the consequences of one's actions will be. Even more important perhaps is the evaluation placed upon the discriminations that are made. For example, the patient, and unwittingly the analyst, participate in a peculiar assumption which makes for mutual distrust. The patient is either openly or tacitly concerned with the meaning of the analyst's acceptance of him in the analytic situation. He suspects that the analyst's acceptance of him is basically dishonest in that the analyst would not accept him outside the analytic situation. It is as if his true self existed on the outside, and that for professional reasons the analyst tolerates him only in the office. Thus, the relationship to the analyst is experienced as an artifact. The fallacy of this attitude is rooted in the paradox of the true self versus the acculturated self. Hence, is the amorous alcoholic presenting his true self—namely, he is really amorous but does not dare express it when sober—or is his sober state his true state of being? This paradox is resolved by recognizing that under certain conditions, a particular facet of interpersonal operation emerges which can have a validity of its own and which correctly regards the paradox as a pseudo-problem. The issue is not one of insincerity on anybody's part, but one of focusing attention more adequately on the solution of problems under set experimental conditions. Value judgments—that is, whether I genuinely like someone or feel genuinely liked—only later become an appropriate focus for scientific inquiry.

The dreamer arrogates to himself the license of irresponsibility just as society has agreed to hold the ill person less responsible. But the dreamer has even broader latitude until inner anxiety puts a wakeful stop to this orgy. In dreams, as in play, one can try something on foresight without being committed to it as a part of one's durable equipment for living. The dream can often be a quite serious, groping, probing, experimental type of process. The dreamer attempts to solve something by allowing his imagination free play, but commitment to action in this context does not have the meaning that it would have in the waking state. The communication in the dream has to be oriented, therefore, in relation to a number of other aspects of living. In the setting of the patient-doctor relationship, the dream illuminates feelings and formulates them more precisely, without their having to be submitted to immediate action.

When searching for the underlying basis of a symbol of any kind, one arrives at a complexus rather than a simple entity. The symbol never hangs by a single thread; rather it is part of a whole fabric. One of the difficulties in analytic work is that interpretations are often made in a linear one-to-one fashion, with particular objects in the dreams being interpreted as meaning this or that separate thing. A kind of digital coding is set up in which the nuances are destroyed. As a result, the significance of the experience in the context of the patient's life and problem is lost. The error of this approach was perhaps more obvious in the early beginnings of psychoanalysis, but it is perpetuated still by all sorts of dissenters as well as the orthodox group. The error, partly practical and partly theoretical in nature, arises from the expansible anlage of the symbol. It is then theoretically multiplied many times through the vast number of probable meanings developing out of the existence of the symbols in the same set, which set may contain nondenumerable possible meanings. Thus all practical dream interpretation must be a highly selective process the operational aspects of which have interested serious students. The impossibility of a simple solution has provoked skeptics to denounce dream interpretation as a dogmatic, self-serving, nonobjective expression of the interpreter. The special problem, however, is to recognize what determines the particular selective process, i.e., what makes the interpreter utilize a particular interpretative scheme.

The latent dream thoughts, under the influence of the dream work, converge at particular points and make for rather simple pictorial display, and are elicited through the association chains, patterns of behavior, intonations, emotional flavoring, and so on in the analytic setting. The practical problem of therapy involves one in a judicious selection of particular trends from the conscious material. The heuristic importance of appropriate dream interpretation is then self-evident. For the analytic interaction to be effective, the analyst must introduce some unique quality into the analytic setting by a spontaneous approach to the dream.

Some inferences and deductions on the psychological processes involved in symbol formation can be drawn from investigations that have been made into states of waking consciousness in which the image also plays an important role— the hypnagogic experience and the daydream. The early works of Silberer and Varendonck in these fields have historical significance in the development of dream theory and will be briefly reviewed here.

The pioneer work of Silberer on hypnagogic phenomena, reported as "an experimental approach to the explanation of dreams," was an early scientific effort to throw light on the image-making faculty of the dreamer and on the conditions which bring it into play. Like Freud and others, Silberer used his own personal experience as the basis for his observations on symbol formation.

The phenomena that he reports, he says, were essentially accidental in their occurrence. He was lying on a couch one afternoon and, though extremely sleepy, forced himself to think through a comparison of the views of Kant and Schopenhauer concerning time. But in his drowsiness he was unable to sustain their ideas side by side. After he had made several unsuccessful attempts to do so, his eyes closed and he was as if in a dream. During this state, he reports, the following picture appeared in his mind: "I am asking a morose secretary for some information; he is leaning over his desk and disregards me entirely; he straightens up for a moment to give me an unfriendly and rejecting look."

In analyzing this experience, Silberer states that it consisted really of two conditions—drowsiness and an effort to think. The drowsiness is a passive condition, not subject to the will; the effort to think is an active condition, manipulatory by the will. It is thus a struggle between these two antagonistic conditions that elicits what Silberer calls the autosymbolic phenomenon. He describes it as an hallucinatory experience which puts forth automatically as it were an adequate symbol for what is thought or felt in a given instant. It is essential, he asserts, that neither of these two conditions outweigh the other; their struggle must remain unsettled so that the scales which measure the relative weight will oscillate indecisively. The prevailing of the first condition would lead to sleep, the prevailing of the second to ordered normal thinking. Thus the autosymbolic phenomenon occurs only in a transition state of consciousness—that is, in the hypnagogic state, the twilight between sleep and waking.

This does not mean that a translation of thoughts into pictures occurs only in the hypnagogic state, for Freud shows clearly in *The Interpretation of Dreams* that this type of translation is one of the essential features of dream formation. Silberer maintains only that it occurs in the hypnagogic state in relative isolation from the other dream-forming factors and that the hypnagogic experience therefore offers distinct advantages for a direct and exact observation of an essential element in dream formation.

In terms of the content symbolized, Silberer classifies the autosymbolic phenomena into three groups: material phenomena, functional or effort phenomena, and somatic phenomena.[2]

The symbols that occur in autosymbolic hallucinations, he observes, are characterized by overdetermination and, since they adhere closely to the psychological experience which precipitated them, they are poor in multiple meaning: "Here the threads of significance emanating from the symbol fasten upon closely neighboring ideas. Consequently, the symbolic

2] This classification does not, we believe, sufficiently stress the role of the metaphor, which also translates thought into picture and describes the form of an idea. The relation between the use of metaphor in waking communication and in dreams can be seen in the following instance of two friends having a conversation in which one tells the other that he is thinking of going into the hardware business and the other replies, "Don't go into the hardware business. Everybody is pulling out of that now. Don't swim against the tide." Now the metaphor here—to swim against the tide—says very concisely that one must follow the trends in business rather than buck them. But the speaker may be implying in addition something which he knows about this friend—that he is the type of person who gravitates toward oppositional action.

That night the man who has been thus advised has a dream that he is swimming against a tide in the ocean and that he is thrown up against the rocks. The dream puzzles him, but he does not recall the conversation about the hardware business. The next day, however, in conversation with another friend, he again says that he is thinking of going into the hardware business. Then suddenly he experiences with some sort of enlightenment the connection between his dream and the previous day's conversation. Here the metaphor used in common speech is "restated" or converted into pictorial metaphor—the conventional form of communication in dreams. The meaning is the same.

relationship (between the symbol and its object or, for caution's sake, its chief object) becomes tighter, more obvious and more definitive. . . ." [3]

The tendency to picturing is a characteristic of symbol formation which, Silberer emphasized, deserves special attention: "When a psychological entity undergoes symbolic substitution it takes on a sensory form, though otherwise it is usually more abstract." He advances the view that in dreams, neuroses, autosymbolic hallucinations and the like, "the symbol appears as a substitute for something [which one] could under normal conditions clearly grasp, think, or feel: a thought which in daytime—assuming an intact psychic apparatus—would be entirely clear, presents itself in . . . dream[s], etc., symbolically." [4]

This view, we believe, is open to criticism in that it fails to recognize that much more is dared in dreaming than during the waking state.[5] The symbol picture during sleep, i.e., dreaming, may be manifestly quite similar to what might occur in the waking state, but there the analogy ends. One must remember that the dream symbols are primarily connected with extensive prelogical thought processes and thus do not undergo the compactness and organization into relevant restrictive channels that thinking in the waking state undergoes.

Silberer infers from his autosymbolic experience that sym-

3] Herbert Silberer, "On Symbol-Formation," in David Rapaport, *Organization and Pathology of Thought* (New York: Columbia University Press, 1951), p. 215.
4] *Ibid.*, p. 216.
5] *Ibid.*, p. 216, n. 47. Rapaport, in examining Silberer's findings, also takes issue with this view: "What presents itself . . . in the dream is—according to psychoanalysis—a thought that could *not* be thought in the waking state: it is always unacceptable and intolerable to consciousness."

bol formation has a great deal to do with a state of consciousness in which one is not in full command of one's ideas. The drowsy state makes one lose to some extent command of one's ideas. Then symbols begin to form as a substitute for the underlying ideas over which one has lost command.

A similar process can be observed in the developmental history of human knowledge, he points out:

> ... *generation after generation, man pursues knowledge through series of images and mythologies—then the symbol appears as a substitute for ideas of which humanity has* no command as yet. *The conditions favorable to symbol-formation may be reached either by advancing toward or by receding from the idea represented by the symbol. Some curious misunderstandings in the literature of the history of culture can be traced to—among other factors—the neglect of the first of these possibilities. The disregard for the second proved a hindrance to the development of psychology and psychotherapy.*[6]

What Silberer describes as the autosymbolic experience corresponds closely to what has often been described as the work of intuitive insight or creative insight. The individual reaches a period of drowsiness, stagnation, or difficulty in thinking and then, as though coming to him, outside his command of it, a vivid image or half-formed idea of the kernel of the insight presents itself to him. From there on he begins once again to take command and to elaborate the half-formed notions or images into the fully formed insight.

When the coordinated contradictory forces to sleep and to solve are not so imperative as in the hypnagogic state de-

6] *Ibid.*, p. 217.

scribed by Silberer, there is another equally interesting state of mental activity, experienced by everyone, that may throw light on the dreaming process. This is the daydream. The daydream is usually a period of abandon to aimless thought and imagery, often tinged with pleasant feelings. Unlike the creative search, daydreaming is released from the burden of achieving an explicit end result. The daydream is implicitly structured with no intent to forseeable activity—no conscious, goal-directed plan.

Perhaps the simplest way to conceive of the daydream is that it is a phenomenon somewhat analogous to the ordinary dream of sleep by virtue of its freedom from restrictive barriers. But even more important, it seems to operate in what might be called a slightly modified state of consciousness that goes in the direction of sleep consciousness. Thus the type of mentation in the daydream is closely allied to that of true dreaming and, like the dream, calls upon the ordinarily more inaccessible sources of inner experience. The significant interest in the daydream and in its connection with regular dreaming, therefore, resides in the opportunity it affords to capture material pertaining to deeper interpersonal dynamics. In one sense, the search for such reveries is not uncommon in psychotherapeutic procedure. Obtrusive reveries are known to occur under circumstances which suggest areas of conflict. Thus, for example, some patients note that they are preoccupied with peculiar thoughts during the sexual act, or they find that their minds wander towards certain types of thoughts when they are listening to a lecture or watching a movie. Intense preoccupations irrelevant to the immediate circumstances are similar to daydreaming.

The extent to which the daydream is similar to the ordinary dream in content and structure is a still unresolved question. The slightly modified state of consciousness in which it occurs is in general so easily converted into the conventional waking state that the threads of the daydream can be very difficult to capture. Any intrusion of critical thought and critical judgment will alter its flow.[7] Our own impression, however, is that the daydream has many similarities with the night dream. Not only are its threads equally difficult to capture, but we are certain that what Freud refers to as *secondary elaboration* also occurs in reconstructing the daydream as well as the night dream. Though it cannot be positively asserted that the daydream and the night dream belong to the same category of experience, it might be scientifically useful to assume that this is the case and then to search for the ways in which they differ.

The literature on daydreams is rather sparse, perhaps because of the technical difficulties involved in recording one's daydreams. However, a significant collection of material on the subject has been provided by Varendonck, and Freud also has a comment on daydreaming in his *Collected Papers*.

In reporting his own daydreams, Varendonck observes that there seems to be an absence of reflective awareness and corrective tendency in the state of consciousness in daydreaming, as in night dreaming, but that qualitative variance of awareness seems to exist. While the conscious ego is suspended, certain types of material can be identified as follows: (1) the perception of an outer stimulus of either a

7] The state of consciousness appropriate to the task of recording one's daydreams is that of the stenotypist, who lets the dictation "flow" from the speaker through his fingertips and on to the machine without "knowing" what he is taking down. In the case of the daydreamer, of course, the percepts come from the subject himself instead of from outside.

harmless or an exciting nature which immediately associ-
ates with a recollection and is soon lost to sight; (2) the
coming to the surface of a day remnant which may be indif-
ferent or emotionally accentuated; (3) ideas which are
selected experimentally and may immediately link up with
memories.[8]

Daydreams emerge, Varendonck states, in connection with
the appearance of a dynamically significant idea, which may
itself arise either from unknown factors or from some external stimulus. (Again, this sounds somewhat similar to
the process of ordinary dreaming.) The material in daydreams, he says, are of two types: material that is primarily

8] In commenting on Varendonck's findings, Rapaport states that the so-
called innocuous ideas are oftentimes the beginning of a dream sequence
and that this has been demonstrated through dream material that has been
induced by hypnosis and also through sensory stimulation in sleep. He
states further that flexible people make use of all means available to bring
them closer to a solution when they are attempting to solve a problem, and
that the difference may be described as one between the limitations of what
is feasible for ordered problem-solving thinking and the nearly limitless
freedom of feasibility in the dream and daydream. Rapaport raises an interesting question with respect to the notion of concentration and voluntary
effort. There is, of course, a paradoxical implication to the whole notion of
free association because one forces oneself to free associate, yet the very
notion of free association implies the absence of force. However, even
attending to the material that comes into consciousness requires some degree
of concentration or of voluntary attention. Otherwise one could not capture
the material coming into awareness. The task of capturing the material
raises the question as to whether the very process of paying attention does
not itself interfere with the free flow of the material. In other words, the
observer once more gets in his own way and may modify the output by his
very presence. Rapaport correctly states that the use of such notions as
voluntariness, concentration, or lack of concentration and so forth should be
considered primarily as descriptive rather than conceptual. The major task,
we agree, is to determine as carefully as possible what processes are identifiable, rather than to decide that a particular process under scrutiny deserves
the status of a theoretical concept.

visual and material that seems to represent verbalization. He claims that the visual type of material is much more closely related to the unconscious while the verbalization type is more related to the conscious levels of the mind.

Referring to one of his daydreams, Varendonck observes that it is composed primarily of a string of suppositions and objections, of questions and answers disposed in pairs, between which there are no very apparent transitions. But, he points out, there is really a common background; a prevalent set of themes keeps obtruding, so to speak, as if there was a goal-directed quality to the daydream. The ever-recurring note is that he wishes to have a particular soldier punished. All the different propositions and counter-propositions revolve around this recurrent expression of anxiety. One can see that he is attempting to solve the problem of how to get a particular task accomplished and that the attempts to solve it involve inventive thought. There is, of course, the simpler situation also in which the daydream is not involved in inventive processes. In such simple cases one often sees only the drive need and the wish-fulfilling thought.

Varendonck finds four causes for the termination of daydreams: (1) external stimuli; (2) internal stimuli arising from a wish to awaken or to sleep; (3) elation accompanying inventions in dreams; (4) conflict with the critical faculty. Actually these causes are perhaps best not regarded as causes in the ordinary sense of the word because what Varendonck is doing is similar to what anyone has to do in the study of this material, namely to pursue where possible what is happening, to follow the nature of the material, rather than to interject an immediate interpretation of what produces the material or how it is modified. Undoubtedly there must be conflicting elements in the form of wishes and perhaps other types of mental phenomenon which allow the person to emerge from the daydream after a certain amount of satisfactory experience has been achieved. The daydream cannot be separated from the state of consciousness which exists. Its interruption or termination occurs when the state of consciousness is altered. External or internal stimuli which disturb the state of consciousness will have the same disruptive effect on the flow of the daydream as emotional forces which operate upon it more directly.

Freud points out with reference to daydreams that the characteristics one may expect to find in the processes belonging to the unconscious system are: (1) Exemption from mutual contradiction and (2) primary process (mobility of cathexis), timelessness, and substitution of psychic for external reality.[9] The coexistence of the conditional "if" with the disregard for it and for time is a coexistence of both secondary and primary modes of thought characteristic of daydreams. Freud also mentions, but only incidentally, the possible bearing of ego attitudes on daydreams. We suggest that ego attitudes are extremely important and that the search for deep underlying drives (although these are also important) tends to throw out of focus types of material which undoubtedly deserve to be considered in the hierarchy of important patterns of reaction. To treat ego attitudes as if they were exclusively superficial phenomena is not only unwise in itself, but probably brings one to the familiar fallacy of reduction.

The processes involved in fantasy thinking are obscure.

9] In Freud, "The Unconscious," appearing in the *Collected Papers* (New York: Basic Books, 1959), Vol. 4, pp. 98–136.

Freud saw these processes exclusively in terms of drives and defenses against them, just as he did in night dreams. Certainly further study of these processes would be fruitful.

Daydreams often succeed in allaying, at least temporarily, the fears and urgings with which they deal. Their work of planning by experimenting with possible solutions seems to succeed at times in considerable relief of tension. It has often been observed—as Freud has observed with reference to mourning—that an undigested experience is slowly digested in the course of brooding over it. There are many observations of this type of mental functioning in which a person reconstructs in his mind what has happened and considers what he might have said or done in a situation which did not come out well. Freud refers to this type of process in describing the behavior of children who, when they return from the doctor's or dentist's office, play doctor or dentist. In so doing, they "digest" the unpleasant experience by working it through bit by bit, adjusting themselves to it and relieving themselves of whatever tensions it has created. Obviously this is partly a magical process, but it has sufficient connection with reality so that it can serve such a function. Perhaps the significant element in this process of correcting situations either in daydreams, dreams, or in play is that the correction is not directly involved with reality. Rather, it implies that something different *might* have occurred. And it fosters the hope—and the intention—of playing in any future challenging situation the role in which one has seen oneself in his reveries.

A function of image-making is to resolve the vast manifold of complex referential processes many of which operate below the level of awareness and many of which, if appropriately discovered, would penetrate uncanny experience in the private domain. However, it is crucial to appreciate the broader implications of entering the private domain whose activity is not exclusively concerned with danger. On the contrary, as Piaget among others has pointed out, responding to a threatening situation does not unleash only defensive referential processes but also creative potential.

4

Symbolization & the Maturation Process

IT IS a common observation that, in the process of maturation, we largely lose access to the quick, intuitive processes that operate with such rich imaginative and inventive
activity in the early years of childhood. This may be what
the poet Wordsworth means when he speaks of "the glory
and the dream" fading into the light of common day as
"shades of the prison house begin to close upon the growing
boy."

Obstacles in the way of man's fertile rapport with his
deepest inmost nature have been described by many people:
by Rousseau as social conventions that distort and repress
the "natural" man; by Freud as inhibitions or repressions of
biological instincts; by Wilhelm Reich as resistances against
the affectively important recollections from infancy and early
childhood; by Sullivan as security operations addressed to
maintaining the esteem of others; by Fromm as self-alienat-

ing bondage to irrational authorities; and by others, each according to his own emphasis and his concept of the inherent nature of man.

Sullivan and Freud, among others, have emphasized the inevitability of these obstacles as inherent in the process of maturation in a social environment. Sullivan said, "Let us be very clear about the fact that anxiety and security-operations are an absolutely necessary part of human life as long as the past shall be more important in preparing the young for life than is the reasonably foreseeable future." He adds, "But for all their indispensable utility, security operations are a powerful brake on personal and on human progress."

The importance of the cultural heritage, the past, in preparing young people for life is already obvious in the relationship between the infant and its mothering-one. It becomes more explicit with the employment of language behavior. As Lawrence Frank points out, "Every language expresses a conceptual formulation of the world and how it is believed to operate. Thus the structure of a language—its grammar, syntax, vocabulary, use of verbs, etc.—implies the basic assumptions of a culture about the world, how the events of it are related and how the speaker participates in it." [1]

The human being, insofar as he is human, is one with the culture, however rebellious, however defiant, nonconformist, or original and creative he may be.[2] But, as he is also separate

---

1] Lawrence Frank, *Individual Development* (New York: Random House, 1955), p. 43.

2] "Culture is mediated through persons, and a culture or a profession, or a level of administration, or a point of view cannot be represented by a chart, or a diagram, or a printed description, but only by living human beings who themselves embody the (cultural) position which is to be taken

from the culture, he must resolve this peculiar human paradox. He accomplishes this resolution by a radical criticism
of himself and his culture. Like the great poem, which
transcends the formal structure and logical meaning of language by an individual illumination of emotional truth, man
transcends his culture by actualizing his innate inviolable
given-ness of true feeling through fertile communication.
Man has the capacity for feeling and showing this feeling
as part of simply being alive, over and beyond mimicry and
social forms. That true feeling is given can be seen even
when man is born deprived of a critical sensory part of his
human equipment. For example, Jane Thompson reports
that congenitally blind children show the complete range of
human expression: "Laughing, smiling, crying, anger, fear,
sulkiness and sadness," she observes, "all have basic neuro-
muscular patterns which are *innate* in the human organism
showing themselves in blind and seeing children, and apparently modifiable by the maturation process. The voluntary
control of the emotional expression which is learned through
social mimicry and becomes habitual probably develops between the ages of four to sixteen years." [3] (The mimicry and

---

into account. . . . Careful analysis of the habits and practices of a people
shows that the traditional behavior such as between parents and children,
for example, is systematically related to practices which obtain between em-
ployers and employees, audience and actor, teacher and pupil, etc.; and that
the way in which a dwelling-house is perceived is related to the way in which
one's own body is perceived with various degrees of specificity, elaboration,
and intensity. This systematic or patterned quality of culture is a function
of the integrated character of human beings who, as they incorporate
cultural traits, sometimes very diverse in origin, organize them into viable
ways of life." From Margaret Mead (ed.), *Cultural Pattern and Technical
Change,* UNESCO (Paris, 1953), p. 308.

3] Jane Thompson, *Development of Facial Expression in Blind and Seeing
Children,* Archives of Psychology, No. 264, 1941.

control probably occur earlier than Miss Thompson states, and are concomitant with the development of awareness of one's self, we believe.)

The human meaning of a situation is that which is experienced through emotional rapport with the situation; and this rapport is a function of very complex intrapersonal and interpersonal reaction patterns, the dynamics of which need not be registered in awareness. Piaget, who has minutely studied the development of human consciousness from earliest infancy, states:

> *Just as there are motor schemas and intellectual schemas, so there are affective schemas (which are the same schemas, or at least indissoluble aspects of the same reality), and it is the organized set of these schemas which constitute the "character" of each individual, i.e., his permanent modes of behavior. . . . Affective schemas are less susceptible to generalization and abstraction than intellectual schemas. . . . At the level of spontaneous, nonregulated feelings, affective schemas can only correspond to intuitive intellectual schemas, which means that they do not achieve logical or moral generalization and abstraction. An intuitive thought is intermediate between the image and the concept. It represents only by imagining, in contrast to logic, which represents by deducing relationships. In what is imagined, the general is always replaced by a particular case, substituted for it not only as an example, but as a participation, or in a strict sense, as a "substitute."* [4]

The development of these affective schemas in the course of a person's growth is the emotional development of that person.

4] Jean Piaget, *Play, Dreams and Imitation in Childhood* (New York: W. W. Norton, 1951), pp. 188–9.

The symbols which give substantive concreteness to emotive forms of experience are therefore not mere epiphenomena; they are expressions of a meaningful, identifiable aspect of human maturation. Thus the dream, with its superficially random, disorganized, arbitrary characteristics, gives potentially valuable indications of meaningful structuring by the dreamer of his emotional maturation and his capacity for interpersonal interaction.

Symbolizing activity also has broader implications which go beyond the scope of this book but which nevertheless are an important backdrop to an understanding of dream phenomena—factors which inhere in the human situation and which modify certain specialized functions. The details of the earliest forms in which feeling and thought take shape are a vital part of this backdrop.

Something of the earliest development of an individual's awareness can be inferred from observations of neonatal and infantile behavior. For example, the awareness of some kind of distress can be inferred from the emotional expression of the infant. His emotional expression matures and differentiates with the maturation and differentiation of his sensory-motor organization. At first he may react to any noxious stimulus with his whole being, moving his extremities violently, crying, breathing heavily, emptying his bladder and rectum, and dorsi-flexing his back. As he matures, his behavior becomes more differentiated and his response to stimuli more discriminating. His experience has prepared him for recognizing; that is to say, the repetition of events in his life becomes patterned. The central nervous system has begun to register for the future certain invariant aspects of the series of events in his life.

This patterning of recurrent events or aspects of events is the beginning of memory and thought as well as of awareness. Hot and cold, breathing and not breathing, are probably some of the first enduring patterns of experience in awareness and thought. Another configuration might be the vague image of a nipple; recognition in regard to this nipple would occur as the purposeful, meaningful discrimination of the nipple from the surrounding environment. Knowing the nipple would express the relationship between the noted external object nipple as anticipatory to satisfying experience; in a hungry infant this would be a cue for sucking. Piaget says,

> *The nursling, from the second week of life, is capable of finding the nipple and differentiating it from the surrounding teguments; therein is proof that the schema of sucking in order to nurse begins to be dissociated from the schemata of empty sucking or sucking at random and thus results in recognition through acts. So also, after the first to the sixth week of life, the child's smile reveals that he recognizes familiar voices or faces whereas strange sounds or images astonish him. In a general way, every functional use (hence all primary circular reactions) of sucking, of sight, of hearing, of touch, etc., gives rise to recognition.*[5]

At this early level of consciousness the infant does not locate his body in space and has no conception of a relativity between the movements of the external world and his own. He does not know how to construct either groups or objects —that is, geometrical or functional patterns of related conceptions or schemata, or enduring conceptions or schemata

5] Jean Piaget, *The Construction of Reality in the Child* (New York: Basic Books, 1954), p. 5.

absolutely dissociated from any action of his own. Therefore, having no capacities for organizing his experience according to the categories of class or for recognizing things as objects in themselves, he may well consider the changes in his image of the world as being simultaneously real and constantly created by his own actions. The nipple may be conceived of as simply an extension of the sucking activity, having no localization in space and no substantial form. The image begins to be created after repeated failures of the initial activity to bring about the object required—such as failure of sucking movements to be completed by the presence of the nipple. This image or picture or concept has enduring relations between its parts corresponding to the relations between the parts of the experience itself. Lip-nipple, taste-nipple, and swallowing-milk-nipple are probably separately represented in this earliest development of consciousness. Gradually, however, through eye-mouth, eye-hand, eye-ear, and other sensorimotor coordinations and associations, the infant's universe becomes separated into his own sphere of activity and a substantial permanence existing independent of this activity.

At first there is no substantial enduring object as we know it, but merely a series of totalities and positions, such as papa-at-his-window, papa-in-front-of-one's-self, papa-in-his-chair, etc., so that although all the different papas are known as one and the same person, the infant will look for him in two or three places while at the same time knowing he is there beside him. Later, from about the end of the first year onward, the infant will recognize visible displacements and dissociate his body and the external object or person from the immediate context. He will eventually recognize papa wherever papa may be perceived, without looking for him else-where at the same time. However, even then, he cannot imagine or represent in mental activity the movements of the father outside of his perceptual field. When the father has disappeared behind the door, he can only be imagined as existing in relationship to this door.

In the next later stage, the infant may imagine the father walking in the hall towards the door or down the stairs to the street; he now has represented in his consciousness the autonomous character of the father; he is aware of the father as a substantial enduring form through a variety of positions and contexts completely separate from his own activity and perception. Pari passu with this, the child develops aware-ness of representations of his own body in space and time, and the parts and functions of the body in relation to each other. Aspects of this body schema become permanently in-corporated simultaneously with the creation and develop-ment of the self, as an enduring "I-am-ness." Paul Schilder, who has done a great deal of research on the relationship between the body image and the self, says: "The postural model of the body is the basis of our identification with others. Whatever makes a change in our experience about our own body is, at the same time, a social phenomenon." [6]

One of the earliest experiences of well-being and security in the infant's life is probably that of breathing adequately in a warm place after birth. Another is probably the satisfaction of the adequate and appropriate sucking-nipple-milk-swal-lowing totality. If one in the series of these particular totality experiences should include an emotional state of severe

6] H. S. Sullivan, *Interpersonal Theory of Psychiatry* (New York: W. W. Norton, 1955), p. 113.

anxiety in the mother, the infant may react with a disturbance of his feeding activity as though his organism were trying to cope with a nonflowing, depriving, threatening nipple-milk schema. This is a signal for avoiding that nipple and seeking another one or for rejecting that milk as a harmful substance.[7]

The very worst experience in the universe of the very young infant one might imagine as a state of being unable to get *any* relief from the *most* severe tension from all his various modes of activity. This must be an experience of total chaos. If this state is unrelieved eventually by any more satisfying state, the infant experiences apathy much like that of the rats described in the Curt Richter experiments:

> *These rats had survived initial poisoning . . . that had made them very ill. Subsequently, when given a choice of two cups —one filled with poison, the other with unpoisoned food— although they were able to recognize the unpoisoned food they became suspicious of the unpoisoned food as well. At the height of their reaction to this choice between poisoned and unpoisoned food they stood motionless for hours on their hind feet in one corner of their cages; partly supporting their weight . . . [they] maintained these postures for months, except when disturbed or when they ate or drank.[8]*

Infants deprived of essential mothering have frequently died of marasmus.[9] Fortunately, most adults feel and are rela-

7] In the sixth Macy Conference on problems of infancy and childhood, a speaker reported: "Babies who continue to cry we can do nothing for and our local pediatricians give them phenobarbital. I have one mother who said, 'I took the phenobarbital myself and the baby stopped crying'." *See* p. 155.
8] Howard Liddell, "The Role of Vigilance in the Development of Animal Neuroses," in P. Hoch and J. Zubin (eds.), *Anxiety* (New York: Grune & Stratton, 1950), p. 186.
9] John Bowlby, *Maternal Care and Mental Health* (Geneva: WHO, 1951).

tively competent to feed and administer to the needs of infants most of the time.

The worst moments the infant experiences probably become a vague prototype of hell and the good moments probably a prototype of heaven. As the consciousness, the memories, the imagery, the representations of the infant's body and that of the adult become differentiated, localized in space, discriminated in proportion and quality, and known as separate, enduring, substantial forms, the prototype of heaven probably becomes personified in a Good Mother; and the prototype of hell in a Bad Mother. At this stage of development the child might cry, "Mama!" seeking the Good Mother when frightened by a severely distressed Bad Mother. Later the Good and Bad Mothers become fused in a personification of one and the same mother enduring through a variety of contexts and positions in space and time. Sullivan says, "Now this personification is not the 'real' mother—a particular, living being considered as an entity (by us adults). It is an elaborate organization of the infant's experience." [10]

At some time after the sixth month and before the eighteenth month, the infant creates by means of his personifica-

10] Similarly, Sullivan points out, "The mother's personification of the infant is not the infant, but a growing organization of experience 'in' the mother which includes many factors only remotely pertaining to dealing with this particular 'real' infant. . . . Part of what he symbolizes to her is her recognition of these responsibilities. What these responsibilities are vary somewhat from one family group to another in any particular community, or in any particular culture area. The degree to which these social responsibilities are effectively discharged may vary greatly in the same mother with respect to different children or with respect to the same child at different times." H. S. Sullivan, *Interpersonal Theory of Psychiatry* (New York: W. W. Norton, 1955), pp. 112, 113.

tions of himself and others the Self which begins with me-nipple, me-Mama, me-Papa, etc. This occurs pari passu with the development of negative personifications such as not-me, not-Papa, not-Mama, and the development of language behavior. The Self has, so to speak, taken over the function of awareness in relation to expression and communication. The infant gradually bars from communicative awareness much of the data associated with calling forth the Bad Mother experience. What is not barred remains as signs for varying degrees of anxiety. These signs are elaborated during the course of a lifetime of learning ways of satisfying one's needs and achieving security without getting into too much trouble with others. Diminished anxiety is sought in the pursuit of the approval of others—in the pursuit of admiration, appreciation, respect, prestige, and so on; increased anxiety is avoided by avoiding the disapproval of others—their contempt, condemnation, hostility.

In the course of what may come to be adult maturation, one develops the capacity to endure the severe anxiety aroused by the disapproval of others in order to achieve what is most important in full human living. Maturation involves the emergence of the individual human identity, the awareness, the consciousness, the experience of one's self as a separate whole individual human being, free to participate in a wider universe. This freedom is an expression of one's knowledge of one's continuity with the ground through which one has emerged.

We have been attempting to indicate that maturation operates in different areas of man's living. From a common-sense standpoint, we are all relatively clear about the nature and conception of maturation. However, our particular emphasis deals with the nature of symbolization as a potentially maturing process. As we have been demonstrating, the processes involved in symbolization maturation are manifestly different from what we would anticipate in the common-sense domain of maturation. We are all agreed upon certain lines of development in the symbolization process. Thus, in living with one another we are obliged for better or for worse to suppress certain autistic processes which if permitted to operate in awareness unchecked would unquestionably create serious disturbances in the social scene. There are many ways to describe how the socialization or acculturation processes reveal themselves. Freud has formulated his conception in one set of constructs and Sullivan, as another example, has presented a formulation which ideologically differs in striking ways. However, Freud, Sullivan, and other students of human nature would agree that the individual, by a vast assortment of techniques, is molded successfully or less so into a social being. The forces which are brought into play to effect socialization or acculturation appear to go in a linear direction. The infantile must be suppressed or eradicated, and the adult must be encouraged or forced into achieving adulthood. Our argument with this sketchy statement of maturation rests on the recognition of an oversimplified and distorted conception of maturation. Thus, we show that the early referential processes that are creative in nature unfortunately undergo serious suppression, which not only limits creative thought and action but also limits satisfactory pleasure and curiosity in ourselves and in others. If these early processes did not have to undergo such suppression we might not only find ourselves more imaginative and creative but we might also exchange our boredom and manipulation for a genuine affection and concern for those around us.[11]

In this book we purport that we must discover and foster the emergence of those prelogical processes that are crucial to being alive, to recognizing aliveness in others, and to establishing a therapeutic milieu analytically that would nurture the rich inner resources of man's nature. This is a dangerous process simply because being alive has always been dangerous. Clinically, we have come to learn that it is not man's hostility and man's guilt that are the most obstructive dynamisms but that the fear of knowing oneself and the other person and the fear of loving and being loved are man's greatest threats.

11] Ernest G. Schachtel, "The Development of Focal Attention and the Emergence of Reality," *Psychiatry*, XVII, 309–324.

5

The Human Situation as Reflected in Perceptual Experience

THE PSYCHOLOGY of perception confronts the investigator with two troublesome existential variables peculiar to man: (1) the phenomenon of introspection and (2) man's innate neurophysiological equipment whose functioning "violates" expected physical laws.

There have been two basic approaches to the study of perception: the physicalistic method and the phenomenological method. The physicalistic method deals with what is commonly called the *facts*. These facts are assumed to exist in the public domain. The phenomenological method, on the other hand, aims to explore how one experiences a percept. These two aspects of perception frequently require no distinction in experience. The things that we see and the **way** these things strike us are often obviously the same. Thus **a**

66

great deal of our living imposes no need to check scientifically what we perceive. However, the science of perception has shown that the physicalistic and the phenomenological methods of perceiving do not coincide throughout. Optical illusions, for example, illustrate that the appearance of things may differ quite markedly from the facts of things. Experimental psychology has gathered important data on optical and other sensory illusions in areas where introspection might enter.

It is clear that a science of perception must explain the phenomenological aspect of perception since it is this method of perceiving that is the untutored, spontaneous approach of all human beings. A science of perception which fails to explain how things appear to us and why they appear as they do is inadequate.

A further component complicates matters; complex neurophysiological elements or aggregates play a very important role in perception. Thus perception is not a simple process whereby one can extend projection lines from the viewed object back to the retina and expect that such projective schemas would clarify the nature of the perceptual experience. Furthermore, emotional factors, stresses, and the particular setting in which perception occurs influence what we perceive and how we perceive it.

Yet appearance and reality seem to coincide for man in an extraordinarily large number of instances and man's tendency to error is strangely small when compared with the opportunity for error. Man's remarkable capacity to perceive an object correctly even under virtually impossible conditions suggests that the process of perception is not exclusively a physical process. For example, it is often possible to know the true hue of an object despite the presence of conflicting colors and despite varied types of lighting. In other words, we are able to compensate, up to a certain point, for conflicting perceptual experience. There are other peculiar qualities of man's perceptive apparatus, often taken for granted, which enable him to make use of types of mechanical devices that would be useless to him were it not for the fact that his physiological reactions operate in the way they do. For example, we can see moving pictures because we automatically "fill in" motion where there is no motion. We "create" three-dimensional phenomena while viewing two-dimensional pictures in a stereopticon. There is no way of explaining these phenomena on a purely physical basis. The theory of optical projection, with respect to lenses and so forth, does not elucidate how man is able to make the necessary perceptual corrections and adjustments to what is actually dealt with.[1]

Let us turn our attention now to another facet of the perception enigma. Psychologists have for many years recognized the existence of an introspective component in perception. The fact that introspection is in essence a private experience introduces serious difficulties in a scientific endeavor in which objectivity is allegedly an indispensable factor. Objectvity is something highly to be desired because it increases the possibility of sharing with someone else a set of observations uncontaminated with private reactions. It is a part of man's inherent maturation as a human being, whereby clear and accurate communication between different persons is made possible. But with the development of objec-

1] See Floyd H. Allport, *Theories of Perception and the Concept of Structure* (New York: Wiley, 1955).

68

tivity, there can also be a loss of appreciation of certain processes in the human being which are not yet and may never be amenable to the objective formulation of conventional scientific method. Therefore, when confronted with experiential data of this type, there has been a tendency to avoid such study or to construct an "as if" experiment.

For example, one of the methods used in studying perception has been to have a subject observe a particular percept, to make certain comments, and to act in a certain way in relation to the percept. Then a second observer observes the first observer and simply records whatever he is able to observe; his recording is regarded as an objective statement about how the first observer observes the percept. In principle, the use of such a method as this was believed to obviate a good deal of "private" information, that is, introspective data.

The weakness of this particular method, as we see it, seems to be twofold. First, if one deletes material that comprises a part of perceptual experience but that is not congenial to a particular method of study, one has actually distorted the very problem one has set out to explore. Secondly, the second observer has his own private reactions that operate while he is observing the first observer, but he acts as though these reactions do not play a role in his observation of the first observer. This type of experimentation either implicitly treats the observer as if he is a nonphenomenological individual who reacts or responds only to the facts or the conditions of experimentation, or the conditions of experimentation are designed to neglect the phenomenological aspect of perception.

As a science of perception should explain how we experience things and why we experience them as we do, any plan, procedure, or experimental approach that explicitly or implicitly avoids the task sidesteps the question. Even if there is no immediate solution, let us see at least whether we can identify the real dilemma which we are describing. In the first place, we set out to solve a problem; but then in all sorts of ways, devious and otherwise, we attempt to by-pass it, whether we recognize what we are doing or not. The clue to this paradoxical behavior resides in part in the history of the development of scientific method and our worshipful attitude toward the traditional scientific approach. Among its postulates, scientific method requires objectivity. Ideally, objectivity means that personal elements do not influence or modify the project under study. Private reactions are reduced to a practical minimum and all experimental procedures are set up so that they can be consensually validated.

Objectivity is unquestionably one of man's most valuable qualities. It represents the capacity for transition from a non-communicable self to a communicable interaction with others. Yet a dogmatic and unimaginative devotion to objective method can be a curb to creative thinking and feeling. The restrictive function of objectivity must be constructive, not inhibiting. Justifiable limits must be set, otherwise the mystery of man cannot be an object of continuing inquiry. Uncritical worship of objectivity closes off access to the heart of this mystery through the intuitive, prelogical processes which man employs to communicate thoughts and feelings that lie too deep within himself to be given logical formulation in language.

It is interesting that, despite the precision, consistency, and rigor called for in mathematics, the vital element in mathematics is man's creative intuition. Hilbert's theory of the formalized structure of mathematics is essentially based on intuitive procedure.[2] In some way or other, openly or hidden, even under the most uncompromising, formalistic, logical, or postulational aspects of procedure, constructive intuition always remains the vital element in mathematics. Does not this really mean that, despite the capacity for rigor and formalism which is possible in the exact science of mathematics, fundamentally there has to be present for genuine understanding and growth a type of process referred to as creative intuition? Irrespective of what man touches in living, irrespective of the degree to which he wishes to place his discoveries in terms that are formal and rigorous, there is always the steady current of man's creative intuition which nourishes the structure.

The problems connected with explaining how one comes to the thoughts one has are still unsolved. No one has yet understood clearly how the mind operates in the creative elaboration of mathematical processes. And how we come primarily to understand what particular direction our own spontaneity takes when we are listening to a dream is equally obscure. Once the creative process has been launched, it can be exposed to objective scientific desiderata. But the formalistic approach must not be initiated too quickly lest one crush the beginnings of a creative notion which arises in a nonformalistic, nonpropositional form.[3]

2] R. Courant and H. Robbins, *What Is Mathematics?* (New York: Oxford Univ. Press, 1941), p. 88.

3] In this connection there are many situations in ordinary experience which demonstrate that much can be reacted to more effectively if consciousness does not prematurely share in the perceptual experience. There are many

The basic error in applying scientific method to a study of these qualities in man, whether in studying perception, dreams, or other borderlands of this type, is that one uses the physicalistic method in an improper experiential sequence so that one actually attacks the problem with tools only appropriate to a later phase of the particular task. Thus one employs procedures which are designed for direct encounter, for measurement, for public process, while the experiences under investigation contain much of what is ordinarily considered subjective and even unique.

Let us explore what there is in the nature of emotive experience, art experience, and perception that might allow us to see more deeply into the problem of studying these types of essentially inner experience. If two people read a poem which, in its essence, is extremely subtle, metaphoric, and primarily evocative of feeling tones, and if these two people seem, as far as one can describe it, to be in emotional agreement on the message of the poem, what does this mean? It must mean that that which is in one sense a strictly unique inner experience can be shared with somebody else. This suggests a paradox itself; if the reaction to the poem is a unique experience, can it be shared by anyone else in the same way?

Possibly the paradox in perceptual experience is rooted in

---

illustrations, for example, of man's capacity to register perceptions accurately in space and time categories provided that conscious cognitive processes are postponed. With this knowledge of man's superior judgment when using his precognitive capacities for certain tasks, the army trains its artillery observers to utilize those capacities to the utmost. The observers must always call the position of a shot as quickly as possible—there must be "zero delay" between noting the fall and shouting out the location. All beginners wish to estimate with the aid of rational judgment, but experience has shown that there is unquestioned superiority of performance when rational estimation is suspended. The first flashing quick guess turns out to be the best guess.

the paradox in man himself—his contradictory capacity both to experience something uniquely and at the same time to share this experience under some conditions with someone else. This paradox operates more significantly on the syntactical level. As long as the experience is shared by somebody else and is not discussed in the logical terms of syntactical relationships, the peculiar quality of separateness-togetherness is not recognized as inherently contradictory.

It may well be that the two separate things that have to be reconciled—namely, the unique, private experience and the shared experience—are really only two parts of an identical, unified process and that the shared aspect is the more mature aspect or the fulfillment of the beginning, which is the private experience. One might say the private experience has reached its full growth in the shared experience and that the two are progressive stages in a unity of process.

The dream, even more than the poem, expresses this paradox of interpersonal experience. In its structure, it contains primarily material which does not lend itself to immediate logical operational inference. The rational process is actually at its best when it is dealing with past established structural entities; but when applied to emerging material, to emerging facts, it may actually introduce an irrational note by virtue of the fact that it is not applicable as such to emerging material.

In telling the dream, the dreamer describes his life situation. He not only describes what he experiences in awareness, but much more than he is aware of. The creator himself—he who creates the dream, the poem, the work of art, or the scientific intuition—is often unable to appreciate the full implication and meaning of what he has created. A poet can discover much about his poem from the responses of the people who read it. The dreamer, too, learns more about his dream in hearing the full response of the interpreter to it.

The nature of man and his creative potential and the patterns of his particular way of being seem to preclude the possibility that the dreamer or the creative artist can have an interpretation of his own creation similar to that of the audience. Participant communication is essential to exploit the full value of any creative process. The meaning of participant communication derives from the concept of interpersonal experience wherein deep emotional interaction and contact occur. Interpersonal experience is indispensable to human existence. In proportion to such experience one's relation to oneself is purer, richer, less laden with avoidances and with gross and fantasied fears. Man inherently tries to move toward man despite his given separateness. The therapeutic situation aims to facilitate contact with another. The dream is one mode of contact that can be shared productively with a therapist. In dream interpretation what goes on in both participants must be experienced together.

The more the dream creates, the more it reveals life processes. To that extent the interpreter gains a great amount of information about the dreamer; and to that extent it may be increasingly difficult to feed back this information to the dreamer. The problem of unassimilable material is both a theoretical and a practical one. The practical aspect is dealt with by utilizing psychotherapeutic procedures predicated on the assumption that anxiety and defensive activities block the path of that material to reality interpretation. The theoretical aspect of the problem includes the broader human dimension yet to be understood.

Clinical psychiatry has not been unmindful of the existence of subthreshold phenomena, although it has not made an organized attempt to see these phenomena within any far-reaching perspective. Needless to say, many therapists must have worked with them without realizing the possibilities of a structured study of these phenomena. Sullivan, in his outstanding work with schizophrenics, perhaps exploited subthreshold communication in the therapeutic situation more extensively and effectively than anyone else has done. But, while using his very great gifts for responding to the subtleties of the other person, Sullivan underestimated the value of this approach for theoretical constructs because such phenomena could not be fitted into a scientific, consensually validatable mold. His writings reveal, however, his tremendous acuteness with such phenomena, despite his intense preoccupation with the formulation of operational statements.

Sullivan's conceptions of modern psychiatry reflect his preponderant concern with the symbolic process and modes of symbolizing. The prototaxic, parataxic, and syntaxic modes of his conceptual formulation are descriptive postulations of symbolizing states which run a genetic course oriented toward maximal syntaxis with maturation. Sullivan sees the dream as serving a homeostatic function coordinating with certain beneficent biological properties inhering in the sleeping state. The functional importance of sleep, in Sullivan's view, derives from the relaxation of security operations.[4] This permits many of the unsatisfied needs of the waking state to be partially resolved during sleep by the covert operations of the dream.

Because of the serious limitations involved in dream reporting, Sullivan was often prone to underestimate the importance of dreams. He regarded the sleeping state as one in which experiential and referential processes are of a different order, precluding the use of rational consensually validated communication processes. He implicitly conceived of communication as being in the syntactic mode. Thus dream reporting, which is almost a hopeless process, cannot be redeemed through the channels of conventional language, which is itself violated by the very task imposed on it.

Sullivan deals with the dream in practical terms by allowing its over-all themes to evoke in him a significant message which he may then report to the patient. When a dream does not produce this effect on him, however, he drops any preoccupation with it. In other words, it is not used as a basis of therapeutic or scientific investigation; it is not regarded as an effective tool for the therapeutic enterprise. He

4] This relaxation under the conditions of effective health is controlled by the self-system, Sullivan states. The self-system also operates apparently as a homeostatic system in which balancing vectors seem to be self-regulatory within a fairly wide range. If the self-system is overloaded, as not uncommonly in the sleeping state—i.e., if significant experiential processes cannot emerge safely into awareness—a serious strain is imposed on the self-system balance. The "rupture" of the self-system results in "over-relaxation," so that primitive referential processes break into awareness during sleep and the sleeper awakens in a schizophrenic state. Thus Sullivan says, ". . . we maintain our dissociations, despite recurrent periods of sleep, by maintaining continued alertness, continued vigilance of the dissociative apparatus in the self-system. As a derivative of that, it may be said that the more of personality which exists in dissociation, the less restful and more troubled will be the person's sleep."

listens to the dream report in the way he might listen to the report of any waking experience, interrupting only to clarify possible ambiguity or misunderstanding. He is not interested in its separate elements. He makes no claims on the patient's free association. In fact, he warns strongly against free associational methods with certain patients, since much of the dream material is acted out in dissociated parataxic experience. After hearing the patient's dream, he states what he has distilled, stripping the dream of its irrelevancies and its obscurities and presenting the patient with something of the patient's way of living. In other words, the dream is used to illuminate for the patient what has been going on in his life, what the threats are in his living, how he deals with these threats, what his various security operations are, and so on. Sullivan ascribes to the dream a source of relief for unsolved problems in living; the dream maintains the parataxic process for this purpose.

Notwithstanding, Sullivan recognized the occasional wisdom of the dream. He states in brief:

> *Both the myth and the dream represent a relatively valid parataxic operation for the relief of insoluble problems of living. . . . The dream has that function for a person in an immediate situation, but insofar as he remembers it and communicates it, he is seeking validation with someone else. The schizophrenic illness . . . is the situation into which one falls when, for a variety of reasons, the intense handicaps of living are so great that they must be dealt with during a large part of one's waking life in the same dream-myth sort of way. Insofar as schizophrenic content, reported dreams, or personal myth are stripped of some decoration in the telling, and thus undergo to some extent the general process of consensual vali-*

77

dation, the dreamer, the schizophrenic, or the myth-maker has some awareness of aspects of his life problems that have hitherto been utterly prohibited from such awareness by security operations. In these terms, such content can be dealt with in therapy; but to deal with it on the basis that one can convert dreams or myths into consensually valid statements by intellectual operations seems to me such a misunderstanding . . . that I don't know how one can take it seriously.[5]

Sullivan's position seems confusing for the following reason: On the one hand, he indicates that it is possible in listening to the dream to strip it of a great deal of its disconcerting, irrelevant, misleading content and to arrive at something which might be a consensually validated statement concerning the dreamer's way of living; on the other hand, he indicates that one cannot, through intellectual operations, expect to convert dreams into consensually valid statements. Perhaps Sullivan raises the question here as to what constitutes effective dream interpretation with respect to the therapeutic situation. He cites, for example, a dream in which there are sufficient data in the dream itself and sufficient data derived from the communications of the patient about relevant matters in his life to allow one to make, with a high degree of probable correctness, an inference concerning the meaning of the dream. If the intellectual operations of dream interpretation consist in literal equations of dream elements with other symbolic elements outside the dream or simple decoding devices, nothing would be achieved. A more complex process is involved in that the listener's intellectual,

5] H. S. Sullivan, *Interpersonal Theory of Psychiatry* (New York: W. W. Norton, 1955), p. 342.

imaginative, and emotional resources are often widely called upon to grasp the message of the dream.

Despite the obscurity of dreams and our lack of full underderstanding of the processes involved in dream interpretation, we are still able under certain circumstances to determine what dreams mean. And we cannot avoid their study. It seems, however, that the syntactic process, which is an aspect of scientific objectivity, achieves its effective stature only when the nondiscursive preverbal presentational mode of experience remains the source material for what later becomes organized thought and discursive communication. If we apply the test of physicalism and phenomenology to the dream, what are our expectations of arriving at a constructive evaluation of the dream? Perhaps it is important to recognize that the more that human experience reflects the private domain of living the less accessible is it to physicalistic methodology. It would appear for the time being that we must rely heavily on the phenomenological assessment of the dream and other presentational forms of experience because by their very nature these processes, as distinguished from other perceptual experience, afford us very little opportunity for discursive inquiry.

6

Subthreshold Phenomena in the Perceptual Processes

THE PROCESSES which operate to permit or guide the specialized human responses expressed in selective inattention are essentially not understood. To say that a person has "perceived" something which induces him to give it no conscious attention is primarily a statement of an end point, rather than a description of process. For clinical purposes we have assumed that selective inattention is initiated by covert anxiety operations since there is a wealth of data to verify such an assumption. Nevertheless, we do not in truth understand the mechanisms involved. To spell out somewhat schematically what we are attempting to identify, let us say that we note that some threatening or anxiety-provoking communication has been perceived by the person whom we are observing because he has seemingly paid no attention to it. There is no reason to believe that his sensory equipment as such is not functioning appropriately; on the contrary, it appears to be functioning extremely well because he is able to get the threatening message and, without even knowing that he has received it, carry out the necessary operation to deflect the threat.

Any attempt to demonstrate to the person himself what has happened would be met with strong resistance, amounting essentially to a denial not only of the missing pieces but of the fact that the event had even taken place. This ubiquitous phenomenon can be illustrated by the following instance: One day during a supervisory conference the therapist had brilliantly reported the content of several recent sessions with a patient, describing a resistance trend which culminated in the patient's request to cancel a forthcoming hour. After this presentation, a tape recording which had been made of these sessions for purposes of research was played back in the presence of the therapist. The recording showed a curious discrepancy between the facts and the therapist's report of them—it was he, and not the patient, who had canceled the forthcoming hour. But until he heard the recording the therapist would have, as he put it, vigorously insisted that it was the patient who had done this.[1]

Selective inattention is presumably both a physiological process designed to restrict the perceptual input within manageable limits and also, of course, a process concerned with managing security operations—that is, operations designed broadly to protect the person from anxiety. If the sensory input is too great or too small or if it is threatening to security, a form of altered perception is called into play. The term selective inattention is applied to this altered perception when it relates to psychological stress. The terms sub-

1] Personal communication from Lawrence S. Kubie.

threshold perception, subliminal perception, or subception refer generally to nonpathological processes. But all these forms of altered perception have in common the registration of the percept within the psychobiological organization and the failure ordinarily of such perceptual experience to emerge within awareness. It would appear that the state of consciousness of the individual is intimately connected with the phenomenon of subthreshold operation. These types of situations which diminish the state of normal consciousness, namely sleep, severe head injury, and isolation experimentation, provoke the operation of subthreshold perceptual activity. Perhaps it is wiser to say that the subthreshold perceptual activity manifests itself more obviously or is more easily accessible to observation in states of diminished consciousness. The state of consciousness from the waking state to the sleeping state appears to be gradient in its nature. There seem to be periods of slightly diminished consciousness which are provoked by physiological over-stimulation or under-stimulation or psychic stress. In this state of consciousness the subthreshold percepts emerge more apparently in the presentational mode. It is with this hypothesis in mind that we shall review valuable recent clinical and experimental studies on subthreshold perception, personality changes in brain-damaged persons, and the effects of isolation on the individual.[2]

The complex truth about man's unconscious perceptual

2] The entire problem of subthreshold perception has controversial implications. See, for example, J. C. Naylor and C. H. Lawche, "An Analytical Review of the Experimental Basis of Subception," *J. Psychol.,* XLVI, 75–96.

functioning has been strikingly demonstrated by recent experiments in which the perceptual processes of the normal person in his waking state have been studied as subthreshold phenomena. The results of these experiments indicate quite powerfully the amazing connectedness between man and the outside world. They reveal, furthermore, a vast communicational process inherent in man's nature which has been unexplored so far.

Needless to say, subthreshold perception is an ongoing process covering a broad spectrum of different states of consciousness. The subthreshold processes are, so to speak, busily engaged in picking up huge packets of sensory input and in sorting, filing, and organizing this input in ways that defy understanding. Scientific discovery and verification of this important aspect of man's inherent equipment open up new and promising possibilities for extending our understanding of essentially nonverbal, dissociative aspects of human functioning.

The work of Fisher in this field, which takes off from Poetzl's original researches on the relation of perception to dream material, is particularly significant.[3] With the aid of a tachistoscope, Fisher has demonstrated that in the process of preconscious visual perception, an enormous amount of intricate visual material can be registered psychically with almost photographic accuracy in time intervals as short as ⅟₁₀₀ to ½₀₀ of a second. That the material has been registered can be demonstrated by various tests (the examination of dreams and of drawings, the examination by the patient

3] Charles Fisher, "Dreams, Images, and Perception," *J. of Am. Psychoan. Assn.*, IV, Jan. 1956, pp. 15–27.

of pictures and his selection of the particular picture that was so briefly exposed). But, except under experimental conditions, this material is not accessible to awareness.

Fisher shows further that these visual percepts, preconsciously imprinted, can play a significant role in the structuring of the dream. "It is entirely possible," he asserts, "that the dream work cannot compose a new visual structure any more than it can a new speech.[4] In many of the experiments, every single detail of the visual structure could be traced to preconscious visual percepts of the day before."

Memory pictures from the past do not appear in dreams, Fisher finds, unless they are "covered" by recent sensory precepts: "Even, for example, when a figure from the past does appear in the dream, it can be demonstrated that fusion or condensation with a figure in the tachistoscopically exposed picture or with a visual percept from the scenes surrounding the experiment, has taken place." Thus, he concludes, "The need for day residues in dream formation may be due to the fact that only recent impressions have the capacity to be aroused to hallucinatory intensity." The evi-

---

4] "What Freud said about speeches and verbal material in dreams has to be extended to include the visual structure of the dream," Fisher says. "He was always insistent that speeches in dreams were taken from auditory percepts of the day before. He showed how the dream dealt with these in the most arbitrary fashion—tore them from their context, mutilating them, accepting one fragment, rejecting another, and often fitting them together in a novel manner. He stated that the dream work cannot create a new speech. It is somewhat puzzling why he did not apply the same formulation to visual percepts. . . . He indicated that when verbal ideas in the day residues are recent, actual fragments of perceptions, and not in the expression of thoughts, they are treated like concrete ideas and become subject to the influence of condensation and displacement. In the sense in which Freud used the phrase, it is entirely possible that the dream work cannot compose a new visual structure any more than it can a new speech."

dence seems to point to a fading of preconscious visual percepts beyond restitution after a 24- to 48-hour interval.

Occasionally the preconscious percepts appear undistorted in the manifest content of the dream, Fisher reports, but more usually they undergo the transformations and distortions characteristic of the dream process through the dream work. These take the form, he says, of fragmentations, spatial dislocation, condensation, and composite formation, symbolic transformation, spatial reversals, and rotations. It has not yet been precisely determined whether these transformations and distortions occur during the interval of perception (at the time of the stimulus) or subsequent to the stimulus and at the level of the memory trace, or possibly at both periods.[5] In this connection Fisher cites the work of several investigators who have studied certain aspects of visual agnosia, eidetic imagery, and hallucinations. "In all these investigations," he states, "there is evidence that preconsciously perceived visual or auditory percepts or their memory traces may undergo transformations and distortions . . . in close temporal relationship to the process of perception."

The modus operandi of perceptual synthesis—a still unanswered question—has been dealt with by Fisher as a phenomenon modifiable by psychological forces but not originating out of the psychological matrix. This assumes that the transformations and distortions have taken place during the act of perception and are regarded as "somatic physiological

5] Poetzl, Schilder, and Kluever have assumed this to occur during the perceptual act itself (based on material from patients suffering visual agnosia from occipital lobe injuries). Fisher also refers to work by Bender and Teuber on similar material which "demonstrated such changes as fusions of disparate lines, displacements, and changes in size, shape, and perspective similar to those found in the dream and imagery experiments."

processes inherent in the visual apparatus itself." Although, in referring to Kluever's studies, he cautions against the view that visual spatial factors are basic and independent mechanisms inherent in the visual system, he nevertheless makes a strong case for this view.[6]

An interesting set of side observations by Fisher revealed that, while making their drawings, the subjects unwittingly, automatically would "find themselves" drawing figures appropriately despite conscious interference by corrective think-

6] Fisher cites the work of Narusi and Obonai as lending support to this view. He also cites McGinnis as, among others, having demonstrated that "discriminatory perceptual activity can take place below the threshold for conscious recognition." In McGinnis's experiments, a number of words such as "whore" and "penis," together with comparable words neutral in nature, were exposed below the report threshold. The results showed a significantly greater galvanic skin response to the "unrecognized" tabooed words than to the "unrecognized" neutral ones. McLeary and Lazarus repeated this experiment utilizing nonsense syllables instead of meaningful words. For some of these an unpleasant affect was established by accompanying the first brief exposure of the syllable with an electric shock. When these syllables were later exposed again, the galvanic skin responses were found to be greater for them than for those that had not been accompanied by shock. Even though the exposure was too brief to permit a correct perception, the syllable elicited the autonomic response which had been conditioned to it.

Fisher also describes the ingenious work of Allers and Teller in which normal subjects were exposed to pictures tachistoscopically and on the following day were given a word association test in which the names of objects in the exposed pictures which had not been consciously perceived were used as stimulus words. The subjects were requested to report and draw any images which occurred to them between the stimulus and response words. In these experiments the preconscious percepts were often reproduced with great verisimilitude. Fisher repeated these experiments with some modifications and reconfirmed the results. Furthermore, he conducted six control experiments in which a blank slide was tachistoscopically exposed. In these, he reports, "No correspondences of a convincing nature were noted by the subjects between the drawings of their images and elements in the pictures that were used for exposure in the control experiment."

86

ing—in other words, their behavior was appropriate despite their better judgment.

Fisher calls the type of perception involved in his experiments preconscious, he explains, because although the percepts are taken in and registered outside of awareness, they are capable of being made conscious. But this can only take place under experimental conditions which include control of the field of the day's residues. Fisher states that however useful the process of free association may be in ordinary therapeutic dream analysis, it seems to be incapable of reviving the preconscious visual percepts revealed in these experiments. It has been shown what a large share these visual percepts have in building up the visual structure of a dream. Everyone is aware how many dreams or parts of dreams leave us baffled and how even freely associating patients cannot produce the material which would clarify these obscurities. The evidence suggests that these preconscious visual percepts can be recalled only after a process of confrontation. Even after the subjects make their drawings which so clearly resemble the visual structures of the exposed pictures, they have no awareness of any relationship between them. Only after confrontation and comparison with the original, and then at times after prolonged search, do the subjects note the similarity.

Fisher assumes that a large part of the complex picture that is exposed for only a fraction of a second "may be excluded from consciousness, not because of a selective process, but because the perceptual task confronting the subject is beyond its perceptual capacity." We believe that he fails here to make a distinction between the recording of the sensory data and their recall. His experiments have established rather conclusively that considerable data can be recorded that will not be available for recall under any circumstances, although the fact that this material has been recorded can be demonstrated through the experimental situation.

This suggests that, on a larger scale, something of this sort goes on throughout a person's life, that there are many moments of recorded data in the course of a person's daily activity to which he pays no attention. These do not necessarily conflict with his interests and ways of life, but they are available to him for his creative elaboration in thinking, imagining, and in dreams without his knowing that he had been exposed to them.

Fisher believes that his work demonstrates that those factors customarily regarded as influencing the dream are similarly operative during the waking state; that the dream of the night is already germinating in the preconscious perceptual experience of everyday living; and that these percepts may even lend their form to the structure of a dream many nights later. His experiments dramatically point up the continuum of preconscious perception and its provision of form and structure for man's emergent inner self.

The scientific demonstration of subthreshold perceptual activity as an inherent aspect of mental functioning provides a basis for a new approach to an understanding of the way in which the prelogical processes operate. Processes such as dissociation and selective inattention imply that man has the amazing faculty of taking in and reacting to situations below the perceptual level. One must first recognize before one can dissociate or inattend; otherwise these processes could not operate so reliably. In other words, there must be perceptual reaction, preconscious in effect, which takes place in bare fractions of a second, permitting the person to achieve the emotional set of disassociation and selective inattention immediately with a reflex-like spontaneity. The discovery by Fisher of "lost" percepts reveals, by implication, how these dynamisms operate.

The scientific findings on the perceptual processes also have a bearing on the concept of self-awareness. Since the processes involved in the phenomenon of self-awareness are essentially perceptual in nature, the physiological laws of perception must operate in the realm of self-awareness as they do for other perceptual experience. This means that man has the inherent capacity for discerning "I" and "not-I" even before this discernment emerges into consciousness. For example, observation reveals that at about the age of one year or earlier, the infant shows behavioral indications of distinguishing what is part of his body from what is outside himself. It has been customary therefore to infer that the infant is in no sense able to make "realistic" distinctions before this age.

We propose, in contrast, that the distinction was not in awareness but that there was nevertheless an implicit experiential phenomenon, characterized by fragmented, dreamy elements hinting at connectedness with the outside world. This connectedness reveals interactions with others and objects despite the as yet undeveloped perceptual recognitions. The processes operative before the emergence of "realistic" recognition can be called the subpresentational mode of perceptual functioning in contrast to the presentational and discursive modes. This subpresentational mode operates throughout life. With maturation the discursive mode of perceptual function comes to predominate in consciousness and interpersonal communication, notwithstanding that the perceptual processes themselves are preponderantly in the subpresentational mode. There is, so to speak, an imaginary line or threshold. Those percepts which are in awareness or accessible to immediate awareness rest above this threshold and are simply called threshold phenomena, while those which must be inferred or extracted by experimental techniques are called subthreshold.

Let P stand for perception. Then the set of all $P = Pi = P_{1, 2, 3, \ldots \ldots n}$. Let the subset of all subthreshold $P = P_s$ (unconscious); and the subset of all threshold $P = P_a$ (conscious). Then $Pi > Ps > Pa$ or $Pa < Ps < Pi$. Man is exposed to Pi, the infinitude of perceptions. Ps represents theoretically all subthreshold percepts and comprises a subset of Pi; that is, unconscious percepts elicitable by experimental techniques. Pa represents theoretically all threshold percepts and comprises another subset of Pi; that is, what is in immediate awareness or immediately available to awareness. Since Pi is greater than the sum $Ps + Pa$, what is left over is not-$Ps +$ not-Pa; thus not-Ps plus not-Pa represents the residuum of potential percepts from Pi which are neither experimentally nor experientially registered.

We are assuming that the data of interaction between "I" and "not-I" in early infancy consists of perceptual experience which is not differentiated with respect to any threshold, since a threshold implies the capacity for discerning conscious reactions, ill-defined or well-defined as the case may be. Between the ages of 6 months and 12 months a threshold is inferred from the infant's behavior. The existential problem of duality, that is, the experience of self-awareness, comes into being when the threshold arises separating self-aware-ness from its subthreshold aspects. These subthreshold aspects of the self may possibly operate from birth or even before.

An interesting question concerns the self-awareness of the dreamer. The dreamer frequently sees himself not as he does in the waking state; he may appear younger or older, larger or smaller, distorted as to gender, and so on. Possibly, some of the subthreshold perceptions of the self are emerg-ing in the dream content. And, possibly, such amorphous forms may be the stuff out of which presentational experi-ence of the self can be created in awareness.

7

Subthreshold Perception in Altered States of Consciousness

F ISHER'S WORK on subthreshold perceptual processes is allegedly concerned with normal perceptual activity in the waking state. We shall now briefly review recent investigations into the operation of these processes in the altered states of consciousness induced (1) by brain injury and (2) by conditions of sensory input deprivation.

Recent studies of persons who have suffered organic brain damage from injury or disease suggest that, in the altered states of consciousness produced by brain damage, a dramatic alteration in the conventional modes of handling perceptual experience is demonstrable. Percepts that would normally remain out of awareness break through the threshold barrier into overt thought, language, and action. These are percepts which ordinarily compose material of the dream. They create no particular distress as such in the patient, despite the confusion and misunderstanding they produce in the observers. Just as the dreamer is untouched by the illogicality and disorientation experienced during dreaming, so the patient in the waking state denies the blatant absurdities of a good deal of his thinking, feeling, and action. However, if the behavior patterns are recognized as dream-like productions, then the "logic" of the dream becomes understandable in them.

One of the most striking discoveries made concerning the nature of the defects of brain damage is that the patient's total personality and the social and cultural components of his living are reflected in the symptomatology of his illness. Claparède,[1] and later Betlheim and Hartmann[2] described these phenomena in their studies of the Korsakow psychosis. Schilder demonstrated similar phenomena in his description of epileptic twilight states.[3]

The symptoms in brain injury are not unidimensional defects, it has been demonstrated, but represent the way in which the person relates to other people and to what is significant in terms of protecting himself against real and fantasied anxieties. For example, denial of illness—which is a common symptom in these cases—cannot be regarded as a simple physiological sequela of head injury but reveals many of the shades of unacceptability which illness symbolizes in our culture. Illness is often regarded as weakness, as avoidance of responsibility, perhaps even as un-American.

1] David Rapaport, *Organization and Pathology of Thought* (New York: Columbia University Press, 1951), p. 58.
2] *Ibid.,* p. 288.   3] *Ibid.,* p. 290.

There is a long tradition in Western culture of intense aversion to any defects, especially in mentation.

Weinstein and Kahn say, in addressing themselves to this point:

> Some motivation to deny illness and incapacity exists in everyone and the level of brain function determines the particular perceptual-symbolic organization, or language, in which it is expressed. The phenomena of verbal denial, disorientation, reduplication and "paraphasia," are not individual defects that can be directly represented in anatomical or physiological terms. . . . The fact that one patient may express an explicit denial and another show a withdrawn kinetic state or altered sexual behavior is related not to differently located lesions but to features in the pre-morbid personality. . . . Thus the various patterns of denial were elicited usually by specific questions and conditions in a particular interpersonal situation.[4]

Three outstanding symptoms in head injury are confabulation, disorientation, and reduplication with an emotional tone of flatness. Careful scrutiny of the symptomatology reveals that there are disturbances in memory and judgment apparently unrecognized by the patient. But, strange to say, these specific symptoms are contradicted by other material the patient produces, suggesting that the defects are not what they seem to be. For example, Weinstein and Kahn report:

> It was evident that the substituted time or place often seemed to express denial of illness or to symbolize some feeling about it. Thus the patient who denied her paraparesis and trache-

4] E. K. Weinstein and R. L. Kahn, Denial of Illness (Springfield, Ill.: Charles C. Thomas, 1955), pp. 123-124.

94

otomy referred to the hospital as "Fresh Air Roller Skating Academy." Another woman who attributed the manifestations of her brain tumor, including a subarachnoid hemorrhage, to menstrual irregularities, called the hospital "Menopause Manor." . . . Patients who otherwise could calculate well made errors involving the year and their age. . . . Even patients who could read the clock correctly were disoriented for the time of day. The patient who reduced the distance of miles to 4 blocks from her home not only gave the addresses of her home and the hospital correctly, but could point out each location on the map.[5]

With even minimal imaginative effort, one can observe in these clinical pictures a type of mentation very similar to that which normally operates in the dream. The various devices of the dream, such as condensation, displacement, reduplication, repudiation of the laws of logic and of space-time, are all present. If the patient were to insert the statement, "I had a dream," just before producing the confabulation, the therapist would immediately recognize the implications of the confabulation. He would recognize that the patient is not suffering from a memory defect, not just trying to cover up or fill in a gap; he is communicating something about himself in the symbology of the dream. The wide range of human interests, aspirations, anxieties, defeats, wishes, and insights that the dream may bring out can be seen to exist in these symptoms of confabulation, disorientation, and reduplication.[6]

5] *Ibid.*, pp. 44–46.
6] Weinstein and Kahn further note (p. 96): "The observation of patients with denial is also helpful in appreciating the significance of certain types of behavior in young children. Thus confabulations about the 'good mother' and the 'bad mother' and the imaginary companion are reduplications in

Could one not say that the head injury induces in some cases the discordant symbology of the dream to make its appearance in the waking state? The patient does not know that he is confabulating or that he is "dreaming" when he confabulates, and the doctor can recognize the confabulation as a "dream" only when he is able to note the similarities in mentation. Confabulation is "dreaming" while one is awake without knowing that one is dreaming, just as the dreamer does not experience himself as dreaming.

In Weinstein's material the total responses of his patients impressively simulate a dream state, revealed particularly by their communications. Their complacency and their indifference to disorientation and bodily malfunction are analogous to the affective state of the dreamer. The type of dream which the confabulator produces by his confabulation is closely allied to an anxiety dream without anxiety.

As the patient's health improves, more appropriate affect

---

which the fictitious person is the symbolic representation of some need or feeling of the child. . . . It is of interest that recent studies in young children by Bender, Fink and Green (1953) have shown a type of perceptual organization in response to multiple stimuli similar to that commonly found in adults with brain disease. . . . Piaget (1951) has pointed out the significance of these forms of language and play in young children as a symbolic system whereby the threatening aspects of reality may be resolved. He cites the symbolic play relating to the excretory functions of the body. At one year and nine months, the child put one open box on another, sat on it and said, 'sitting on pot.' Later her dolls dirtied themselves and at three and a half the feces were compared paraphasically to a finger, a mouse, and a rabbit and given ladies' names. A study of these symbolic patterns in relation to the development of perceptual organization in children should be of value. . . . He feels that the two to four year old does not stop to consider whether his ludic representations are real or not. Similarly, in the patient with anasognosia the need to avoid catastrophe is so overwhelming that he seems not to think in terms of truth or falsehood or logic or illogic, but only in terms of survival or destruction. If a discrepancy is noted it is probably disregarded as trivial or inconsequential."

begins to appear. In other words, an experience that should be frightening can now evoke fear. Affective experiences which previously were organized into behavioral sets composed of emotional flatness and dream-like symbolization (not recognized as dream-like by patient or observer) are now converted into the more rational waking behavioral set with its anxieties, hopes, and fears. With improvement in health, the patient's need to protect himself diminishes; the catastrophic reaction can now approximate a felt and observable experience. It is extremely interesting to note that "after recovery patients were apt to refer to their experience as a 'dream'" and that "dreams were very rarely reported during the period in which the anasognosic delusions were expressed." Could not one venture the suggestion that dreaming, in the usual sense, was not necessary since its function was being taken over by the symptomatology of the waking state?

Weinstein and Kahn report:

> *After restitution of brain function, the patients described dreams in which denial was expressed in patterns of confabulation, disorientation and reduplication. . . . A woman who had previously denied her operation after returning home had a dream in which a friend came home well after an operation. It is likely that one of the attributes of normal brain function is the ability to distinguish a dream as such.*[7]

Similarly, dream-like processes of handling perceptual experience in the waking state have been observed in isolation experiments. Recent neurophysiological studies have established the fact that the sensory stimulus has a further function than that of evoking or guiding a specific bit of be-

7] *Ibid.,* p. 96.

havior; it also has the unspecific function of maintaining arousal, probably through the brain stem reticular formation. For normal functioning, it has been demonstrated, the waking brain depends upon a constant bombardment of sensory impulses to produce a continuing arousal reaction. Moreover, the sensory input must be continually varied in its nature or it loses the power to cause arousal reaction. The brain seemingly not only has to be warmed up, but has to be working all the time.

This condition appears to be a physiological requirement of man's nature. What, then, are the effects of reducing or eliminating the sensory input? Scientific investigation into this question has recently been conducted both in this country and in Canada on subjects observed in a milieu created to exclude as far as possible all visual, auditory, and tactile sensations. These investigations have been inspired in part by previous military and industrial studies on the effect of monotony on human functioning. For example, during prolonged radar observations, it has been found that watchers often fail to respond appropriately despite the absence of any distractions. Such lapses of attention are of serious import to military operations. In industry, it has been generally observed that monotony often leads to physical hazard where persons are employed for prolonged periods on repetitive tasks. This factor also accounts for otherwise inexplicable railroad and highway accidents.

One investigation into the effects of reduced sensory input that has recently been reported in detail will be briefly reviewed here.[8] The subjects were students, employed on a

8] "Effect of Decreased Variation in the Sensory Environment," *Canadian Journal of Psychology,* 1954, VIII, No. 2, 70–76.

24-hour-day basis. For purposes of the experiment they were required to lie in essentially soundproof cubicles with U-shaped foam-rubber pillows enclosing their heads to further reduce hearing. Visual perception was limited by the use of goggles through which translucent light could enter but no patterns; and tactual perception was shut off by the wearing of gloves and cardboard cuffs that extended from the elbow to just beyond the finger tips.

In the early period of reduced stimulation, it is reported, the subjects tended to sleep a good deal of the time. Later they slept less, became bored, and appeared eager for stimulation. They would sing, whistle, talk to themselves, tap the cuffs together, or explore the cubicle. The boredom seemed partly due to deterioration in the capacity to think systematically and productively. The subjects were unable to concentrate on any topic for long. Those who tried to review their studies or solve self-initated intellectual problems found it difficult to do so. They lapsed into daydreaming, abandoned attempts at organized thinking, and let their thoughts wander. Some subjects also reported blank periods during which they were unable to think of anything at all. All of the subjects became very restless, displaying constant random movements, and they described their restlessness as unpleasant. Emotional lability was observed. In general, there was a feeling of some elation at the beginning and later a marked feeling of irritability. It was difficult to keep subjects for more than two or three days, and some left before the testing could be completed.

When the subjects were removed from the cubicles after the experiment, they were at first dazed. For one or two minutes there seemed to be some disturbance in visual perception. Focusing was difficult; objects appeared fuzzy; there was a tendency for the environment to appear two-dimensional; and colors seemed more saturated than usual. Feelings of confusion, headache, and mild nausea were reported. In some cases these conditions persisted for 24 hours after the isolation period had ended.

At regular intervals during the isolation period and again shortly following the end of it, various tests were given. On all of these tests the average performance of the experimental subjects was inferior to that of the controls. The number of subjects included in the experiment, as the observers point out, was too small for the results of these tests to be regarded as definitive. Yet the differences noted do seem to be significant.

The hallucinatory experience which the subjects described was of particular interest. Many of them had the feeling of having a dream while awake, and one of the investigators who put himself through the cubicle test observed a somewhat similar experience. (The visual phenomena were believed to be quite similar to those described for mescal intoxication and those that Grey Walter has briefly produced by exposure to flickering light.) As the first subjects were not asked specifically about these phenomena, their frequency for the experimental group as a whole is not known. However, the last fourteen subjects were asked to report any visual imagery they observed, and all of them reported such imagery.

In general, there were first simple types of hallucinations, which later became more complex. The levels of complexity could be differentiated as follows: in the simplest form the visual field with eyes closed changed from dark to light color; then dots of light, lines, or simple geometrical patterns appeared. All fourteen of the subjects reported these types of imagery and said that the experience was a new one to them. Eleven subjects reported wallpaper patterns, and some also reported isolated figures or objects without a background. Then there were even integrated scenes; for example, a procession of squirrels with sacks over their shoulders was seen marching across a snowfield and out of the field of vision; prehistoric animals were seen walking about in a jungle. There were also cartoon-like figures. One curious fact is that some of the hallucinations were reported as being inverted or tilted at an angle.

At first the subjects were surprised by these phenomena and then they were amused and interested, waiting for what they would see next. Later some subjects found the hallucinations irritating and complained that their vividness interfered with sleep. There was some control over the content of the visual images, for in some cases certain objects were suggested by the experimenter; often in these cases the subject, after seeing a number of other images first, finally saw the suggested object. The imagery usually disappeared when the subject was doing a complex test, such as multiplying three-place numbers, but not if he did physical exercises or talked with the experimenter.

Hallucinations involved other senses too. There were auditory hallucinations in the form of people speaking and the playing of a music box. Kinesthetic and somesthetic phenomena were described. Some subjects observed two bodies side by side. In one case the bodies overlapped, partly occupying the same space. There were reports of feelings of "otherness" and "bodily strangeness." One subject said that his mind seemed to be a ball of cotton wool floating above his body. Another reported that his head felt detached from his body.

In summary, the changes in intelligence test performance and the hallucinatory activity induced by limiting sensory input provide direct evidence of a kind of dependence on the environment that had not been previously recognized. Further experimental study is needed, however, to elucidate the details of this relationship.

Continued research into the nature of monotony as well as its more subtle and easily overlooked analogous states is of great interest for several reasons. In the first place, it calls to attention certain aspects of normal psychophysiological functioning which have not been so far clearly delineated. The findings to date certainly suggest that man is definitely dependent upon a bombardment of sensory impulses, broadly speaking, and that this sensory input must have some varying quality or at least some type of unexpected irregularity. Otherwise, a state of reduced attention occurs. Certainly if the practical problem is to alert oneself, then the conditions which best serve to increase alertness must be determined.

The implications of this work have also a bearing on the therapeutic situation. As far as we know, the inner life of the patient tends to come into awareness more clearly and with less static, so to speak, in a therapeutic milieu that reduces outside disturbance to a minimum. For example, free association is best carried out, so far as we know, in such an atmosphere. But there is the possibility that an atmosphere that is not so totally permissive may be more stimulating to the emergence of inner experience. An attempt should be made to find out what conditions most effectively bring man into contact with himself. Certainly the history of psychoanalysis has shown that there has been too much intrusion by others in the patient's life, too much static. We spend our lives receiving instructions, advice, value judgments, and the like from our families, friends, enemies, teachers, newspapers, and a multitude of other sources. It is to the credit of psychoanalysis that it has recognized much of this intrusion as not only valueless but detrimental to significant change in man. Still the pendulum can swing too far in the other direction—that is, the patient-therapist relationship can develop into a kind of monotonous circular operation. The exclusively circumscribed atmosphere that sometimes prevails in analysis may, like the perceptual isolation situation, provoke trance-like phenomena, and it certainly fails to prepare the patient for dealing with the problems of living.

In the isolation experiments cited, it is clear that the capacity for perceptual differentiation, visual and otherwise, is significantly reduced. Without a frame of reference, no kind of imagery can be appreciated. Failing the customary landmarks, things appear out of focus, fuse, and lack organization. In a loosely analogous manner, the analytic situation can create an atmosphere so lacking in referential points as to interfere with the emergence of basically important material.

The processes involved in living are so complex that the central flow of mental and emotional operations must utilize all the levels of one's mental and emotional equipment. Subsidiary tributaries that do not have an important bearing on this main stream of living will tend to become automatized. This means that the individual constantly establishes closed systems to permit his attention to be directed away from trivia. Closed-system mentation is a very striking given datum which operates in the service of psychic economy. Experiential data are automatically scanned for closed-system processing. This state of affairs is essential to effective survival. Catastrophes may result, however, when closed-system mentation is allowed to enter the field of significant problem-solving, for example, in one's marriage, one's work, or one's analysis. Contrariwise, if tying one's shoes involved open-end mentation, there would not be much time left in the day to solve other problems of living. The fallacy inherent in the radar set-up derives from its organization around closed-system mentation when obviously open-system mentation is essential since the purpose of the radar activity is for problem-solving, for dealing with the unexpected, the novel. To install man as a cog in an automatic corrector device for feedback signals misuses the very nature of man's organization.

Since the understanding of man is rooted in open-end interaction, those activities which wittingly or otherwise block open end processes disturb the very conditions for interpersonal problem-solving. The nature of dream interpretation involves open end mentation which is a part of interpersonal interaction.

In the traditional conception of the patient-therapist relationship where the therapist is essentially uncommunicative, an important danger to the therapeutic enterprise can develop. The remoteness and silence of the therapist plus the "hermetically-sealed" consultation chamber, all designed to reduce unnecessary intrusion, may create a deprivation of important input stimulation. The patient can react to this by a closed-system mentation, vague uneasiness and restlessness, and scattered, random, primary process phenomena somewhat similar to those observed in experimentally induced isolation. Since it is already known that isolation under completely acceptable conditions is detrimental to effective and productive mentation, and only induces uncanny regressive distress, it is essential to avoid creating the very conditions of embeddedness affect [9] when we are aiming to stimulate maturational processes in therapy.

9] See Ernest G. Schachtel, *Metamorphosis* (New York: Basic Books, in preparation).

8

Extrasensory Perception

THE SUBJECT of parapsychological phenomena has not yet found full accreditation in the community of scientific enterprise, and there is a tendency to regard all investigators of such phenomena as either charlatans or painfully misguided persons. These phenomena represent certain types of referential processes in which moments of intimate interpersonal interaction occur. As such, they deserve serious scientific inquiry in the total approach to an understanding of man's symbolizing activity. Their investigation might also throw new light on the processes involved in perception, as well as on occult phenomena themselves.

The way in which extrasensory perception, mental telepathy, clairvoyance, and other occult processes operate strongly suggests that they reflect subthreshold perceptual phenomena. For this reason they are difficult to elicit except under carefully planned experiment. But a large body of data exists indicating that these processes are definitely observed in some people under some conditions.[1]

The flexibility of the perceptual threshold seems to vary from person to person, and the conditions for the emergence of percepts into awareness are still not completely understood. When what seem to be subthreshold percepts enter recognition, they ordinarily do so under special conditions of experimentation, in sleep, or in the setting of serious illness. This must mean that such percepts avoid emergence normally because of still obscure properties of man's nature.

There seems to be evidence that highly creative persons are more mindful of and comfortable with the emergence of subthreshold perception material into awareness than the more conventionally oriented person who "reflexly" disowns any responsiveness to his own emergent inner self. Perhaps for this very reason the creative person nourishes his own creativity. An illustration of this is seen in the story that is recorded about August Kekule, the renowned German chemist of the eighteenth century, and his dream of a snake holding its tail in its mouth. Instead of repudiating this dream as absurd, he sensed that it supplied a notable advance in his attempt to conceptualize certain structural problems in organic chemistry. Through his vigilant attention to his own inner life, the concept of the benzene ring was born.

When the subject of extrasensory perception is given consideration, it is customary to regard the experience as being of an unusual and special type, possible only in certain persons with a unique or at least a special gift. We take the posi-

1] Raynor C. Johnson, *The Imprisoned Splendour* (New York: Harper, 1954).

tion, on the contrary, that extrasensory perception is a universal phenomenon, participated in by everyone. This assumption rests on the fact that all of us unwittingly "capture" a tremendous amount of sensory input, as the scientific investigations into subthreshold perception have demonstrated. Not all of us, it is true, have the same facility for making these types of experience explicit in interpersonal processes. But the mental telepathic process itself, we believe, is as universal as dreaming, though the phenomena themselves need not be registered in awareness. Like dreaming, we believe that extrasensory perception is a process inherent in man for illuminating and presenting his unconscious knowledge of himself and his relationship to his world.

Freud in 1925 turned his attention rather seriously to the problem of mental telepathic phenomena in a study of the reactions he had observed in persons who visit fortunetellers. On the basis of this study he concluded that psychoanalysis could throw no definitive light on the validity of these unusual mental phenomena. However, he made some interesting observations. The fortuneteller tells her client many things and makes many very definite predictions of things to come. Though these predictions subsequently fail to be realized, Freud observed that the fortuneteller's client is very rarely disturbed by this fact. The reason for this, he quite ingeniously concluded, rests on what had been established in his whole theory of personality. His position is this: the client in some way communicates his unconscious wishes to the fortuneteller and the fortuneteller gratifies these wishes by the type of predictive material that she presents to the client. It is as if the client had had a wish-fulfillment dream; yet the wish-fulfillment dream, usually camouflaged, in this instance is penetrated by the fortuneteller's powers. The censoring process, of course, does not operate and the client gets the satisfaction of considerable wish fulfillment connected with his own private yearnings.

This raises the question of how the fortuneteller is able to get deeply enough in touch with the client to penetrate his unconscious strivings. The answer would have significance for the therapist, for he too seeks to discover the secret wishes of others. Whatever sheds light on how this penetration is achieved—on the nature of such human contact—is important for therapy. The success of the therapeutic enterprise is based on the degree of meaningful contact that can be established between the therapist and the patient. Possibly, then, there is common ground between the fortuneteller and the therapist in the wish to get into extremely intimate contact with another person and to share previously nonverbalized yearnings in such a way that no anxiety is produced—to create a state of pleasant, unchallenged oneness that is sometimes called empathy or rapport.

As we see it, Freud made an important observation when he noted that man's insatiable drive to fulfill his ungratified wishes will lead him to search for illusory gratification uncritically and even to "hallucinate" its fulfillment at the hands of a fortuneteller. But we believe that man has in addition a deep yearning to communicate and to be understood, and that he might use parapsychological experience as a path to the minds of others. Sparse though the psychoanalytic literature is on parapsychological occurrences in therapy, there is impressive evidence that such phenomena are organized for constructive communication in the therapeutic setting. Unfortunately, however, very little serious experimentation has been carried out to validate this evidence.[2]

An example of the telepathic phenomenon in the psychoanalytic setting is the precognitive dream—a dream indicating a knowledge on the patient's part of the analyst's personal life, often correct in minute detail, which could not be conceived of except through the mediation of extrasensory experience. Servadio[3] takes the position that the precognitive dream is an expression of counter-transference —an expression of unresolved emotional difficulties of the therapist. This position was first taken by Hollos, who believed that the patient's precognitive dream is some kind of unmasking process designed to point up the therapist's professional hypocrisy. The situation in which the unmasking occurs is allegedly one in which the therapist is out of contact with the patient during a particularly strenuous period in the therapeutic relationship. Because of this lack of contact, the patient is "forced" to produce a very powerful precognitive dream to shock the therapist and bring him back into contact.

Balint[4] agrees in principle with Servadio's view of the precognitive type of dream. He describes his own experiences and notes that as his therapeutic abilities have improved through the years, he has not had this type of experience.

2] Jules Eisenbud has been one of the few American psychoanalysts who has given serious thought to the role of occult phenomena in the psychoanalytic transaction. See "Telepathy and Psychoanalysis," *Psychoanalytic Quarterly,* XV, 32–87; "Analysis of a Presumptively Telepathic Dream," *Psychoanalytic Quarterly,* XXII, 103–35; "On the Use of the Psi Hypothesis in Psychoanalysis," *Intern. J. of Psychoan.,* XXXVI, Part 6, 1–5.
3] Emilio Servadio, *Intern. J. of Psychoan.,* XXXVI, 27.
4] Michael Balint, "Notes on Parapsychology and Parapsychological Healings," *Intern. J. of Psychoan.,* XXXVI, 31–36.

He too takes the position that the precognitive dream is a counter-transference dream implying an accusation against the therapist. But, he says, analysts in general would tend to disown responsibility for the implied accusation. By the process of projection and idealization, the analyst has exculpated himself from responsibility and has at the same time had the effrontery to regard the precognitive dream as of great scientific interest. Balint himself anticipated the ridicule of his compeers for provoking this type of dream and felt somewhat ashamed to bring to notice his own deceptions; he therefore hesitated for many years to write anything on this subject, but he now feels free to do so.

Certain questions are seriously posed by the precognitive dream. Probably this type of dream is in part a vigorous attempt to establish contact with the therapist and to disabuse him of his somewhat sanctimonious role as the good parent who patiently listens to the poor struggling patient and helps him. On the other hand, there must be in the history of psychoanalytic practice many instances in which the therapist served his patient rather poorly. Therefore, if the precognitive dream operates exclusively to point up the therapist's shortcomings, it seems highly improbable that there would be so few illustrations of precognitive dreams in psychoanalytic literature, the therapist's self-esteem notwithstanding. The data cannot be explained exclusively in terms of counter-transference phenomena. And we still have to understand how the precognitive experience takes place.

The experiences of thought transference phenomena, like dreaming, seem to arise *de novo*. The person has these experiences without any special effort on his part. Study, will power, and the learning devices commonly employed to achieve mastery play no role in them. The transference may be facilitated by arranging conditions appropriately, but still one cannot provoke such experiences as one can set about mastering a foreign language.

In effecting the results of extrasensory perception experiments, interaction of the experimenter and the subject is of basic importance. In other words, interpersonal factors modify performance and cannot be left out of the equation, thus showing once more that man's relatedness to his fellow man is not just a sociological phenomenon but a basic datum about man. This property of relatedness has a strong bearing on man's capacity to respond selectively to the complex perceptual manifold around him.

9

An Inquiry into the Therapist-Patient Relationship

W E HAVE been emphasizing throughout this book the existence of prelogical processes inhering extensively in man's nature and comprising the vast backdrop to every variety of human experience. We have also proposed that a scientific methodology designed to understand man and cure man dare not neglect, minimize, or take for granted this essential quality in man. To what extent have the practitioners of psychotherapy met this challenge? How has the prelogical manifold been constructively utilized in the therapeutic milieu?

Freud's basic conception of the process of therapy was rooted in the idea that it is the patient who cures himself. This idea is a radical one, for in the history of medicine the therapeutic situation has never elsewhere been defined in terms implying that the patient's collaboration is crucial to the outcome. In the conventional sense of medical treatment, it is quite evident that the patient might usefully follow the doctor's instructions; but in the sense in which Freud discusses therapy, the patient's participation in his own therapeutic venture is essential.

Freud conceived of the therapeutic situation as one in which the patient, given the proper conditions, has the potential for producing information about himself that will bring his own undisclosed self into awareness and thus lead to his cure. The therapist's task is to facilitate the patient's confrontation of himself. To accomplish this task, Freud recognized, external and internal stimuli that oppose the emergence of material must be obliterated as far as possible. Thus the use of the couch, conducive to relaxation, became an important part of the therapeutic equipment. The therapist's office must have a minimum of distracting elements. The atmosphere must be structured to reduce the admission of distracting percepts. Both by his attitude and his comment, the therapist himself must minimize conventional social exchange. Hand-shaking, greetings, gestures of reassurance, simple pleasantries are to be avoided. Reassurance of any kind is definitely contraindicated. The therapist must not be the judge, the adviser, or the moralist. All forms of personal contact are forbidden.

In such a setting unconscious thoughts and feelings are believed to be given optimal opportunity to emerge uncontaminated, through free association. The patient is, in fact, asked to observe only one rule, namely, to cooperate by permitting himself the freedom the theory calls for—to say anything that comes to his mind and to censor nothing. The analyst's function is to aid in enforcing the rule of freedom. One additional therapeutic prescription is to be followed by the patient—that he will not "act out." Briefly, this means that he will not change jobs, get married, get divorced, etc., while under therapy. (Needless to say, there are many forms of acting out which can be extraordinarily subtle and escape the attention of both therapist and patient. This very important issue will be dealt with in greater detail at a later point.)

Freud's policy of noninterference was no trivial therapeutic device. As Freud saw it, the truth about man was bubbling under the surface. His sense of craftsmanship dictated his structuring of the therapeutic situation to provide for the emergence of this unconscious material. But, as Freud quickly discovered, there were serious obstacles interposed to its emergence. In the first place there were the patient's organized defenses and resistances; and in the second place the emergent material required interpretation. Freud strangely believed that the patient's understanding of himself would coincide with the conceptual framework if the patient's resistances and defenses could be resolved. We use the word "strange" because it seems axiomatic that the meaning of inner experience to any two people need in no way be correlated. At any rate Freud recognized that interpretation was needed. Otherwise there would be no rational utilization of the emergent material. Freud used interpretation sparingly—at least he advocated its sparing use. He urged that the therapist wait until the patient is ready to grasp the meaning of his own productions. Nevertheless Freud was obliged to make interpretations and did so consistent with his own conceptual framework.

For Freud the truth that bubbled under the surface was

the vast arena of instinctual forces struggling with counter-forces. These instinctual forces with their opposing tendencies formed the workshop of the therapeutic enterprise. Man attempts to achieve gratification of these impulses by unconsciously structuring all human interaction in such a way as to pattern it in line with his earliest childhood experience. The transference operations of the individual serve that very purpose. Freud saw that these transference reactions would occur in the therapeutic relationship—in fact, it was essential that they flourish powerfully there in order to illuminate sharply the patient's unconscious quest.

Freud's whole conception of man's emotional problem prescribed the quality of the doctor-patient relationship. As a logical outgrowth of his theory, the doctor operates outside the interaction with the patient. The doctor is the observer. The patient's relationship to the doctor is organized around the assumption that it will be unreal. The doctor in turn is alleged to present nothing of his real self to the patient. Ideally, he imposes none of his needs on the patient. Thus, for example, instinctual needs such as falling in love with the patient and ego needs such as the desire to be worshipped and admired have no proper place in the therapeutic enterprise. The doctor's values, interests, personal affairs, or needs for reassurance must not enter into the relationship with the patient. In the training and supervision of candidates in psychoanalysis, the importance of obliterating any needs the candidate may have in respect to his patients is strongly emphasized.

In principle, at least, the conditions established protect the patient from the subtlest exploitation by the doctor. However, they introduce a different set of difficulties for which there are no completely convincing solutions at the moment. These difficulties are several in number. Experience has shown that a person rarely, if ever, interacts with another person without exposing an assortment of needs of his own. Obviously these needs will not be transparent ones, because flagrant violations of intimacy or personal involvement are not really the problem. What one finds usually is that the therapist may make rather subtle claims on the patient and then subsequently get involved in complicated hypocritical denials of his own operations, thereby confusing the trajectory of the doctor-patient relationship. In the extreme sense the doctor acts as if every attitude the patient maintains toward him must arise out of the patient's transference system.

Another highly significant problem that is posed is that the patient is not encouraged by this procedure to be responsible to understand the true nature of the analyst. Since analysis in principle should concern itself with increasing man's genuine understanding of himself and other people, the analytic workshop should encourage a realistic preparation for this activity in the outside world. As we see it, it is essential that the patient penetrate the personality of the therapist. Otherwise the patient has not revealed sufficient growth to qualify for termination of treatment. Furthermore, if in the protected situation of analysis the patient still does not dare to utilize his own perceptual grasp of the analyst, such failure does not speak well for the patient's emotional maturation. Fears labelled incestuous, or in any other way that one desires, block a realistic appraisal of the other person; and needless to say this is no goal of psychoanalysis.

117

The third difficulty with Freud's position is its exclusion of affective reactions of the patient for the therapist as well as of the therapist for the patient. Why do we have to assume that the patient's emotional attitudes toward the analyst can never have any reality, or that his positive attitude toward the analyst is always childish dependency or some form of negative transference? It would seem that we truly reject the patient when we fail to recognize his growing capacity to feel love as well as other forms of emotion toward us. In effect, we recapitulate the very conditions in the lives of the patients, many of whom have never been treated as if their emotions had any substance. Their love, their fears, their anger have never been taken seriously except insofar as these emotions became a nuisance to their parents or teachers. They have never been able to distinguish in themselves that which is genuine and sustaining from that which is false and melodramatic. If they have ever had a problem with authority, the analyst's aloofness intensifies this problem.

And what about the therapist's attitudes? How can they be formulated in such a way as to avoid self-criticism or criticism by others? Growing up in the medical tradition, the doctor feels correctly that his personal attitudes should not interfere with his sincere pledge to help mankind. In the general course of medical practice, very little challenge is posed. In psychoanalysis Freud's theoretical position allows one to maintain objectivity because one deals there with force diagrams. Thus one can hide easily behind the scientific procedure. If one does not have that scientific procedure to hide behind, however, the question that is posed concerns the type of attitude the therapist shall have conducive to the growth of the patient. Do we have to like all our patients? Can we like them all? What does it mean if we do or do not? What does it mean if we have an aversion to a patient?

These are difficult questions to answer, partly because we therapists often do not know what we feel, are embarrassed by what we feel, or feel that we should not feel anything except some kind of benevolent neutrality. We are suspicious of any accented feelings toward the patient, suspicious of the existence of some threat. So in general our attitude toward the patient often becomes extremely difficult to clarify, let alone publicize. If we find that we are not feeling or doing anything in violation of neutrality, we usually have no anxiety. If, however, we receive cues of one kind or another inconsistent with our security-oriented definition of the therapist's attitude, we begin to wonder what this means. Some have the courage to learn something from these cues. Others deal with them by selective inattention.

In general, the real feelings of analyst for patient and patient for analyst have to date received scant attention in psychoanalytic literature. Whatever the reasons for this—and there no doubt are many—some of the avoidance of the subject arises from sincere doubt of its relevance. Traditionally the kindness, dedication, and humanity of the old country doctor have been held before the medical profession as the ideal. But the analyst knows that under some conditions these qualities may perpetuate a dependency pattern in the patient. Any trends toward this type of involvement, even if not acted out, become a source of strain since the analyst has been taught to regard such experience as indicative of unanalyzed needs. Perhaps, however, present procedures in psychoanalysis are too exclusively directed toward avoiding this danger. While playing safe, we may be neglecting to utilize a real and valuable form of patient-therapist interaction which can widen the area of investigation and lead both patient and therapist to a deeper understanding of the patient's life problems.

A fairly common dilemma in the therapeutic situation is the quite formidable opposition to constructive interaction that certain types of patients present. Their work in the therapeutic setting can be serious and diligent; yet the quality of distance they introduce would make even the most remote analyst feel isolated in his office. As the tradition of psychoanalysis assumes that the analyst's intrusion into the patient's realm is unconstructive, the therapist is confronted with an impasse in these cases where the very heart of the patient's neurosis is his subtly disguised isolation from significant emotional contact with anyone. These types of patients provoke one to question whether the therapist is not merely meeting the patient's disguised detachment with his own professionally accredited detachment.

In our therapeutic experience this paradox has often baffled us and has presented us with a discouraging stalemate. We have suspected that the impasse results from theoretically imposed restrictions on the therapeutic potential of the analytic process. Freud's system by its very structure inadvertently blocks the free play of preconscious processes even though that is the last thing in the world it was designed to do. But in some way this vestal-virgin atmosphere of sensory deprivation deprives one of the very emotional situation required for getting into contact with ourselves and with our patients.

In working with patients we observed the emergence in ourselves at certain times of a strong affective reaction; there were also marginal reveries accompanied by a vague feeling of urgency. These unsought-for experiences commanded our attention. Although one could easily recognize counter-transference implications in them, we had a faint suspicion, almost a hunch, that these experiences might conceivably represent a source of contact. It was as if the "prohibition" of other than conventional channels of communication could not suppress these forms of contact entirely. Would it not therefore be important to explore once more those phe-nomena, regarded as counter-transference, as a different order of phenomena implying or reflecting communicational processes so far improperly understood and largely unat-tended to?

Patients whose defensive activities stubbornly prohibit analytic interaction offer formidable obstacles to therapeutic improvement, let alone cure. Yet these patients rarely glimpse even their grossest opposition to interaction with the analyst. Reasonable efforts at clarification of the situa-tion, fortified with carefully planned illustrations of what the patient is doing, achieve little change. These patients meet one's efforts with relentless defiance, which does not appear to be experienced as such by them, but which can eventually try the therapist severely. For example, one pa-tient in our experience, a young engineer who was uncom-monly sophisticated about psychological matters, insisted that he should "do" his own analysis. The analyst's comments were frequently designed to notify the patient that the meaning of his communications had not been made clear. The analyst would frequently resort to the device of metaphor to check his understanding of a particular incident he had been listening to. The patient completely misconstrued these efforts to attain a deeper grasp of his problems. He would respond to them scathingly, treating the analyst as if he were a little boy tugging at the patient's trousers and pleading for attention. With this attitude the patient failed to recognize that he was allowing no genuine experience of rapport. Thus he maintained unwitting distance by the defense of patronizing and paternalistic "wisdom."

The obligatory role-casting whereby the therapist became the insignificant, frustrated, clamoring son in the presence of the great all-wise father graciously tutoring him precluded any opportunity for the therapist to reach with his patient a valid consensus on the patient's operations. Every attempt to impress upon the patient the precise nature of his obdurate repudiation of useful interaction was met with mounting exasperation at little junior's troublesome insistence.

The analyst had a growing sense of helplessness in the situation, for the patient's defensive tenacity was of such magnitude that it would crush the most valiant demonstration of reliable, established modes of therapy. And, little by little, this sense of helplessness blended with a sense of angry frustration. The analyst was obviously confronted with the task of dealing with this stalemate in the analysis as well as with his own sense of helplessness and anger. Although any significant manifestation of anger on his part could be attributed to counter-transference reactions, this whole experience powerfully posed the question: How can the analyst fulfill his therapeutic responsibility under these conditions?

With due recognition to the possibility that a different analyst might have dealt with this particular patient more effectively, the analyst sincerely felt that the patient's defensiveness would defeat the skill of even the most talented analyst. It occurred to him that some other dimension of the analyst's potential for interaction with the patient might be brought into play. Could there be a valid way of acting out by the analyst that would be productive at this particular phase of the interaction? Might not the analyst's anger itself serve as a temporary essential bridge for contact with the patient? Despite a risk, foreseeable damaging consequences did not seem likely to result from expressing the felt anger at this rigidly entrenched personality.

On the basis of this conviction, the analyst angrily talked the patient down. And it was only when he finally expressed his anger in no uncertain manner at the patient's blatant obstructionism that there was some prospect of improvement—some yielding of the rigid barriers to therapeutic penetration. The patient had always made previous analytic interaction completely artificial. His view of himself and of the analyst was entirely at variance with the analyst's view. He saw himself not as an obstructionistic, domineering, self-centered parental figure, but rather as a diligent, obedient, supine boy, only too likely to fall under the hypnotic spell of the serene, all-wise, benevolent analyst. This comforting picture was jostled whenever the analyst opened his mouth, at which point the patient would assume his domineering, suppressive manner.

The emergence of this pattern was not experienced by the

patient as suppression of the analyst but merely as his dutiful desire to free-associate uninterruptedly. Thus, as long as the analyst was quiet, there was no clash, but also no movement. The analyst was to be kept in his place by the flattering role assigned him. The patient, in turn, disclosed precious little to expand his grasp of himself, since he was diligently occupied with warding off anxiety by corrupting the spirit of the analytic process—namely, by accepting no help from the analyst, by resisting any interpretive comment, by proclaiming repeatedly that every smidgen of insight came solely through his own efforts. He was comfortable only in his travesty on the analytic process. Any variation on that theme exasperated him to unleash invective. He never sensed his underlying anxiety since his anger impressively disguised that affect.

This type of patient provokes the analyst, but this provocation is only part of a much more self-defeating program which has to be dealt with therapeutically. However, as we see it, the analyst must eventually engage the provocation rather than transcend it. To assume that engagement is a useless playing into the patient's defensive needs is erroneous, for it misses the gateway to a more deeply entrenched desperation and hopelessness which must be faced.

It is imperative, for example, that the patient be allowed to experience the impact of his operations upon the other person. Such experience in our culture is frequently blurred by the other person's need to establish his own invulnerability and serenity in the face of provocation. Our culture puts a high value on maintaining poise and composure even at the expense of self-respect. It is useful under some conditions in the laboratory situation of psychoanalysis to respond naturally to the interminable provocation of the patient.

In this particular case the patient sensed the mounting irritation resulting from the abusive immobilization that he imposed upon the therapist. His change in strategy was expressed first by the attitude that he was entitled to behave in effect with complete license. Nevertheless the analyst stuck to his guns and showed the patient in strong terms that he would not consent to this type of tyrannizing. The patient was forced to confront something in himself which he had ingeniously sidestepped for the most part in the outside world. On the rare occasions when he could not avoid somebody's sudden explosive fury, he was deeply wounded and bewildered. In fact, his subsequent work in analysis began slowly to represent significant inner and outer experience which seemed to be a response to the more comprehensive emotional challenge of the analyst. He did not experience the analyst's anger as a defensive, impotent response to his long-standing distancing maneuvers.

The underlying issue here is not an emphasis on random expressions of spontaneity, but rather on a scientific inquiry into the potential usefulness of spontaneity under certain conditions designed to increase the seriousness and vitality of the patient's own efforts in the direction of improved mental health. The analyst's spontaneity brings out the patient's spontaneity. Then one has a refreshingly new path to pursue, which leads to more fruitful empirical results than our exclusively academic deductions about ego strength. In other words, we find out whether the patient can grow or whether his defenses are imperturbably rigid. The analyst wants to know such things as validly as he can. If the patient can follow through, mutual hope is stimulated; if he cannot, at least we are not involved in hypocritical verbalisms.

In presenting this clinical illustration, we are not simply saying that it is important for the analyst to express strong emotion at any time or another in his therapeutic endeavors. Nor are we saying that the expression of strong emotion by the analyst is a novel contribution to therapy. Undoubtedly many competent analysts have at times used personal expressions of emotion in their therapeutic work—in some cases with constructive effects and in other cases, no doubt, with unconstructive effects. The real issue is the scientific study of the potentially important dimension of the therapist's emotional spontaneity. Such a study will bring us to the doors of various old and also new aspects of knowledge about the conditions of man's nature in interaction with others.

10

Counter-Transference as Subthreshold Communication

I T IS a commonly accepted tenet of pedagogy that the mastery of a particular human skill is best taught by constructing a simple practice situation, similar to the ultimate test situation, through which the pupil picks up little by little the dynamic clues and cues which enable him to adjust himself to the task. If a child wants to learn to ride a bicycle, for example, he must at some point struggle with capturing his balance on the bicycle. In the beginning someone is at his side to reduce the possibility of unnecessary injury while he is acquainting himself with the nature of his task. But the assistance given him must not overprotect him, or the very information which he must perceive to utilize his own capacities is withheld. We have taken the position that anonymity for the therapist creates new problems perhaps in part conducive to an unrealistic structuring of the patient-doctor relationship. Because of its unreality, this relationship serves as a poor teaching model for the tasks of living imposed upon the patient in the outside world.

Psychoanalysis is a learning experience which calls for teaching. The art of the great teacher is difficult to define in completely discursive terms; yet it includes an incentive to teach, a mastery of the subject, and an indispensable sensing of where one should or should not intervene. Obviously, the maturity of the teacher's personality has a significant bearing on the end results. If the teacher has a strong need to be worshipped and the student can learn submissively, the results of the transaction may be only partially satisfactory in that the student's incentive to learn is subordinated to his incentive to act out an immature pattern of relatedness.

Is not the real issue one of attempting to identify as precisely as possible the optimal conditions of the learning process? Neither of the two extremes—nonintervention or overinvolvement—solves the problem. The solution, in fact, contains a paradox, namely that the teacher shall be realistically involved and yet ideally out of the picture. This paradox cannot be honestly resolved, as psychoanalysis has traditionally attempted to solve it, by denial or restriction of the therapist's personal equation.

In recent years there has been a trend toward a franker recognition of the so-called counter-transference phenomena experienced by the analyst. This has led us to search for a means of dealing with these phenomena. At first we attempted to define away the problem by recommending further analysis for the analyst. But this solution is valid only to the point where counter-transference material is grossly intrusive. The fact is that further analysis is very unlikely to eradicate all counter-transference experience. Two questions come to mind in considering this situation: Must an analyst admit failure because he cannot honestly state that he has successfully eradicated all of his counter-transference reactions? Or must he resort to a white-washing maneuver by claiming that minimal counter-transference reactions cannot seriously disturb the progress of an analysis? The answer to the second question is often temptingly in the affirmative. It is easy to conclude that our counter-transference reactions could not possibly be responsible for failure because the patient's neurosis is so overwhelmingly serious that the balance could not be influenced by the quantitatively small negative contribution of the therapist.

Each in his own way, the analyst with his taboos against his counter-transference reactions and the patient with his unwitting incognito, restricts the input of information potentially useful for analytic progress. There is no question that analytic procedure calls for a constant infusion of new materials, fresh appraisals, and a challenging reconsideration of issues in the light of provocative data. Lacking this quality of spontaneity, the analysis can stagnate; standardized procedures and postulates soon become targets of the patient's resistance. An examination of counter-transference reactions in the analytic setting must not be construed as sponsoring acting-out with the patient, but rather as a serious attempt to expand developmental areas in the therapeutic situation.

Some clinical material in support of our hypothesis will now be presented in which one of us openly brought his own dream material and easily accessible preconscious marginal thoughts about the patient to the patient's attention for response. For purposes of ease in reporting, these experiences will be described in the first person singular, in each instance by the therapist to whom they occurred.[1]

Illustration I

Over a period of several weeks, I had two successive dreams about Patient A which, I decided, might profitably be discussed with him. In presenting the first of these dreams, I pointed out to the patient that I thought it might throw some light on my attitude toward him and I asked him for his impression of it. The dream was as follows:

> *The patient and I are sitting at a small table in a sidewalk cafe, perhaps in Paris. The patient is saying very little, but has a very troubled expression on his face. He appears worried. I say to him, "Why not try to tell me what is the matter?"*

The patient seemed to respond to this dream very meagerly. Except for a polite nod, he indicated no particular interest in giving his impressions and seemed to have something else he wished to talk about. Thus an analysis of this dream was not pursued.

My second dream about the patient occurred several weeks later and was also reported to him:

> *In this dream, he and I are sitting at a table in an expensive bar having a drink. We are talking casually, but the content of the conversation is not recalled. Suddenly, as we are about to leave the bar, two men not previously noticed jump on the patient. The situation develops swiftly, and I cannot tell*

1] Edward S. Tauber, "Exploring the Therapeutic Use of Countertransference Data," *Psychiatry*, XVII, 332–36, 1954, is the basis for the following material.

whether the patient is really being attacked or whether these men are just old friends who are taking the patient by surprise and roughhousing with him. The dream ends as I quickly move to the patient to ask him whether he needs help or whether they are all just joking.

At first, after I had told this dream, the patient made no comment about it except to say that it expressed my belief that he was withholding data and at the same time seemed in need of help. I asked him, "Do you think that I believe you to be in need of help?" He responded rather equivocally, indicating that perhaps he thought I felt this about him.

But later in the hour, he showed by his manner that the dream had something to say to him which was worth considering. His associations implied that the patient-doctor relationship had always been satisfactory and that he felt it was essential to keep it that way, that his experience in life had led him to believe that it was best to let sleeping dogs lie, and that one can never work out a satisfactory solution by getting too deeply involved or by making one's ultimate position known. He then went on to make the important suggestion that both dreams had a hoax-like quality; although they manifestly indicated my concern for him, at the same time he suspected that I was perfectly happy with the friendly, unstressed quality of the relationship; and although I was trying to indicate in a sense that I believed we should go deeper into these issues, I had some private reasons for avoiding the challenge.

I found this latter comment thought-provoking, and I could not answer it with either a flat denial or an affirmation. I seriously asked myself whether I was guilty of wanting to avoid difficulties. My association to this was to remember information from outside sources about the patient that was not very favorable, but I did not feel free under the circumstances to communicate this information to him. I then made some comments in which I indicated that in one sense I believed the dream implied that I was having some difficulty obtaining the maximum degree of participation from him and that possibly the dream was an indirect method of conveying to him my desire for deeper collaboration.

My first verbalized association was that the dream was an attempt to provoke the patient to reveal more clearly the transference picture. I acknowledged the possibility that I might have an unconscious fear of knowing something inauspicious about him and that, although I was not aware of the nature of this fear, it might become apparent later. I pointed out that the dream, in its manifest content, contained a rather obvious message which could be known to both of us. But I reminded him that I could easily have some blind spots about its meaning and that he should develop his own ideas about it.

The next session was an extremely fruitful one because it conveyed to both of us—more strikingly than perhaps at any other time—the essence of the patient's real fear of closeness. It had always been difficult for him to convey the emotional atmosphere of his home situation; although he had previously made sensible statements about it, they often lacked the affect that is so essential in the analytic setting. In this particular instance, however, his usual nonchalance was lacking, and his distress at an impending social engagement was touchingly revealed. After he had expressed this distress, I was able to tell him about a previous occasion when

I had sensed his deep fear of his closeness to his mother. We both then realized that the issue had been hit upon—namely, that I had been afraid to push this particular point for fear of a panic reaction in him. In other words, the dreams seemed to have revealed a pleasant but timid coaxing of the patient, as if I were saying, "One can still go about this matter of one's problems, even while having a drink." Stated in other terms, the dreams were expressions of my ambivalence in that I both urged the patient to greater activity and had some reservations myself about the safety of it.

Illustration II

I had the following dream about Patient B, a young married woman who had been in analysis for a few months:

The patient and I are on an island in the Mediterranean. We are walking together, and there is no conversation. It seems to be dusk. The atmosphere has a romantic quality. I am trying to understand something, although nothing has been said. That is all there is to the dream.

When I reported this dream to the patient, she made no comment. I had decided prior to the analytic session to tell her the dream, although I had not yet considered it carefully myself. When she failed to say anything about it, I noted on the spur of the moment that she did not seem to feel that the romantic components of her marriage were satisfactory, although there had been no mention of it in our work together. I admitted that I had no significant information to justify this association, but it had come to me anyway, and I wondered whether it had any validity.

Subsequently the patient went into the subject of her marriage, revealing that my association had a rather pertinent bearing on her problem. I wondered why this would have to come up in a dream. The patient seemed to have no thoughts on the matter. But it occurred to me that I had been deliberately avoiding the subject of the patient's marriage since she had had so much distress in the analysis and had seemed to have a need to believe that her marriage at least was sound. The dream came to my assistance, however, and prevented my continuing a useless philanthropic attitude toward the patient which could only have delayed the handling of a problem of importance to her. It turned out that her relationship with her husband was not as happy as she wished to believe.

Illustration III

This illustration has to do with a fleeting thought that came to my mind during an analytic session. I revealed this thought to the patient, saying at the same time that ordinarily I would not have done so because it seemed to have nothing to do with the mutual inquiry. I asked him for his reaction to this thought and stated that I would also contribute my own associations. Here is the setting in which the thought occurred:

The patient was describing some details of his marriage. Having had occasional temporary episodes of sexual impotence prior to marriage, he was remarking that he hoped that under the stress of his present marital problem he would not again have the same disturbance. He added that, because he anticipated that his wife would react adversely, such a disturbance would be extremely frightening to him. I had this

134

sudden, unaccounted-for thought, which I revealed to the patient: "Send your wife here to me. I can explain the situation to her in such a way that she won't be disturbed."

The patient quickly reacted to this remark. It revealed to him, he said, that I really lacked confidence in him and did not believe that, if he became impotent, he would be able to work out the problem with his wife. While he was talking, I had the fleeting thought that what I had said seemed to be an expression of ambition, as if I were trying to prove to him that I had the power to straighten out the matter—a kind of credit-taking fantasy. I communicated this thought to the patient. He reacted by looking pale and angry and by insisting that it proved that I was merely trying to deny admitting my deeper feeling of his inadequacy by accusing myself of ambition.

At the beginning of the next day's session, the patient was silent. I urged him to say what was on his mind, but he was still uncommunicative and seemed slightly uneasy and uncomfortable. Prior to this session, I had had some thoughts about his remarks of the day before, and I now proceeded to communicate them to him:

I suspected, I explained to him, that my behavior of the day before represented an unconscious mimicking of the patient's mother or identification with her and that it was motivated by a desire to recapture with him a relationship with his mother which had never come out strongly in the analysis. In other words, I believed that this unconscious device was aimed at forcing him to reveal a sensitive area which could have remained concealed under the ordinary conditions of analysis.

The patient reacted to this comment by blushing and saying, with some anger, "You are trying to get off the hook." By this he meant that I had originally indicated a lack of confidence in him and had first attempted to deny this by explaining my comment as an expression of my own ambition. That failing, I had tried a new tactic—namely, to explain my behavior as an unconscious therapeutic maneuver. But he did not believe that my associations explained away my lack of confidence in him.

At the next session he was quite eager to relate a dream that he had had the night before:

> *There is a huge ballroom filled with couples dancing. A doctor, whom the patient has known for many years and has regarded as an ally of his from early childhood, is dancing with the patient's wife. The dance steps are elaborate, consisting of the partners' stepping away from each other and coming together again. Suddenly the patient's mother, who has been standing alone in the sidelines, gets into the doctor's arms before the patient's wife can complete the steps necessary to bring her back into this position. Apparently the doctor showed no objection to the swift change of partners and willingly continued to dance with the mother. The patient, who observed all this, said nothing, but he was disappointed in the doctor's behavior.*

The patient's associations were that the doctor and I, the analyst, were the same person, and that I had betrayed him. He felt that this dream was his way of expressing what he believed I had meant about our relationship when I had commented on his anticipated potency problem. My interpretation of his dream was in line with his comments. In effect, the dream indicated his feeling that I had turned away from him after having had a satisfactory relationship with him and that I had become an ally of his mother. It indicated that he did feel disappointed in my earlier remarks on the grounds that I had later suspected—namely, that I had unconsciously simulated the patient's mother. In other words, I believed that his remarks represented an unconscious attempt to stimulate or provoke emotional data in an area which was important but still insufficiently explored.

The matter was left with the patient, however, who was urged to attempt to clarify in the analytic work the important critical problem of whether or not my attitude was genuinely hostile. These analytic hours had emphasized for him the necessity of being concerned with my real and assumed attitudes and also the fact that he could not and should not uncritically accept my appraisal of his own attitudes.

Two important points were brought out clearly through this incident. First, the patient was obliged to move away from a somewhat artificially arrived at conception of the analyst's attitude toward him; and he was forced to consider the analyst as a human being with whom he was working, rather than as a special category of person who fitted the patient's defensive needs. Second, the analyst's experiment of expressing a private thought—which, at first glance, was out of order—provoked material reflecting quite genuinely the patient's convincing doubt about his mother's alleged faith in him, a point which he had previously indicated with relatively unimpressive affect.

It is our impression that an explicit interchange can be extremely illuminating for the patient for several reasons. In the first place, one creates a true laboratory atmosphere so that the patient and the doctor proceed with a minimum of mystery or status imbalance. By mutual participation the analyst is able to illustrate what he is refusing to submit to when the patient makes unwitting claims on him. Ordinarily the patient notes the refusal to respond, but does not capture what the refusal is due to; after this, a great assortment of security devices are set into motion by the patient's attempt to regain self-esteem. The illustration about to follow is not designed to imply that the procedures should be followed in a literal, insensitive manner or that no effective growth can occur without following this prescription. The explicitness is aimed to increase the mutually educative possibilities in the human transaction.

Illustration IV

The patient in this case was an attractive middle-aged woman who, after several weeks of therapy, still showed little or no evidence of disclosing her own deeper impressions of what went on between herself and others. Despite her sophistication, great verbal facility, and sensitivity of a sort to conversational counterpoint, it was clearly impossible to decipher her position about anybody or anything in or out of the analysis. When I brought this fact quite carefully and clearly to her attention, she made no response at the time indicative of anything beyond an effort to be respectfully impressed. I further informed her that, if she were able to address herself to this apparently strange phenomenon, a milestone would be reached.

She made no comment on this communication. In general her manner was extremely cooperative and engaging to the point of suggesting unwitting fraudulence. In her carefully controlled, beautifully mannered fashion, she was casting herself upon the analyst, apparently yearning for his help and guidance. She sought a degree of protection which would be beyond mortal powers. This demanding quality was disguised by her sparkle and ingratiation. As she left the office at the end of the hour, she said, in effect, "You know I rely on you and need your help!" This comment was made in such a way that I found myself replying, "The flesh is weak, but we must analyze what you are talking about!" I met her delicate seductiveness in a manner denoting a partial desire to be the knight in shining armor saving the fair damsel in distress.

At the next interview she remarked that she was puzzled by my closing comment of the previous session. I told her that I had found myself reacting to her seductive charm, that I had felt a desire to respond to her flattering request for help. I pointed out that my behavior complemented her desire to stay in hiding. For some reason or other, I said, she did not wish to know what she felt about anything, and her pattern of action had caught me responding in kind; I had for the moment reacted like the fortunate one who would be her savior in return for her flattering, seductive smile. I asked her whether the experience I had just described was not a familiar one to her—that of being able to coax the man into protecting her from her own center of gravity. Her marriage strongly suggested that her husband had in the earlier days eagerly played the role of her protector, her savior, but that he was losing interest in this role. Little by little, he had grown dissatisfied with her, probably because he had discovered that her collaboration was only a charming facade. Since she did not know just what was the matter between them, she would make efforts to recapture the past, but she would find herself increasingly disenchanted because of his failure to follow through in his original role.

I warned her that this could easily happen once more in therapy—that her therapeutic enterprise could easily amount to essentially nothing more than a temporary reassurance at having found another person whom she could charm into compliance with her neurotic needs—and that she must recognize how exquisitely adept she was at parrying any examination of her own attitudes. Her bright intelligence, I pointed out, allowed her to plagiarize without catching on to the fact that such a process was being employed.

She was deeply impressed with the description of her defensive operation, which I had arrived at by permitting myself to feel through what she was doing and to illuminate my own compliance with her neurotic system. She had no feeling of being put in her place, and no objection to the way in which I had disclosed her mode of operation, designed to keep out of awareness her opinions, values, and attitudes.

Illustration V

In this case the patient was a talented, attractive career woman, essentially effective in all her activities, who found herself mostly incapable of lasting relationships where intimacy was concerned. Sexual responsiveness was uncertain, and ill-defined reactions of revulsion, allegedly masked from the partner, were not uncommon. The central problem—neatly concealed from awareness—was a deeply rooted yearning for shelter. Despite a rebelliousness toward Mother, it was from her that she sought everlasting protection. Mother's luxuriant absorption in her blinded her from recognizing a reciprocal pattern. Significant commitment to anyone else did not occur; the quality of her relationships reflected an adolescent fickleness, with a strong need to keep in circulation lest she feel her loneliness. She was acutely sensitive to even the mildest possessive claims of others on her. These claims were rarely illusory since she was almost exclusively drawn into symbiotic contact. In the absence of available opportunity for mutual dependency, she would be uneasy, anxious, and lonely.

For a long period during analysis, the patient did not experience the analyst's "claims" on her even though the form of her communications and certain blank gestures strongly suggested that she believed herself in some danger in the analytic relationship. It seemed fairly clear to me that she was being secretive about much of her experience. Her system required that the analyst be dependent upon her exclusive affection. Thus he must be kept at a distance, lest he feel the threat of her possible interest in others. She anticipated that he could not contain himself were he to realize that he did not mean everything to her. This discovery would impel him to make a captive of her.

I formulated this thesis for her, utilizing what I considered powerful data. She grasped what I meant intellectually; nevertheless she felt that I had designs on making her my captive nurse. But she also regarded her tormenting doubts and indecisions concerning her choice of a marital partner as my sole responsible province. Paradoxically she was aggressive in her mind at my failure to arrive at a perfect choice of partner for her, albeit I was allegedly desperately fearful of her abandoning me. Thus, as long as this strange paradox was not in the patient's awareness and as long as denial operated, the core issues were not being engaged, although the analysis moved at best along quite interesting lines. Fortunately the conceptual framework of the patient's life and of the relationship constructed in the analysis was sufficiently pertinent so that even though the analysis was still more an intellectual than an emotional breakthrough, it moved later into a more genuinely productive direction through the influence of certain unexpected, spontaneous, emotional reactions of mine. A brief illustration of one of these counter-transference reactions will be cited.

Some few years after the analysis had been under way, the patient began to show evidence of a more serious drive to establish a relationship of durability and emotional intensity. The tangled web of forced feelings, remoteness, sentiment, obliqueness, and false discovery began slowly to be disentangled. But with this favorable change there was a growing feeling that I was steering her away from her goal of marriage. In short, she reluctantly brought out the admission that I was threatened by her leaving me. She noticed by my interpretations, my silences, and my manner that I was struggling to deny my need of her and that perhaps, because I had basically healthy intentions, I would not deprive her of her freedom. Yet, in effect, as she experienced me, I wanted to hold onto her. I was no different from her parents. Perhaps her mother was most driven to possess her, but her father too could not release her. Furthermore, the injustice to her was aggravated by her knowing that her parents and her analyst had their own lives satisfactorily in hand. What made them want her to be their little girl forever? Each in his own way did everything conceivable to keep her enslaved. The methods of enslavement they used may have differed, but all were directed primarily to undermining her self-confidence by overprotectiveness, to showing her that she could not succeed in a hostile world and that they would care for her no matter how she floundered about. Her inner picture of herself was that of a little doll in a glass case with a pretty silk dress on and a timid, miffed expression on its polished face.

Then one day when she arrived for her hour, she announced that she had unexpectedly received an offer that morning of an excellent position in another city far from New York. As we talked, it became clear that she was seriously interested in this offer and would probably accept it. Realizing that this would mean the end of the analysis, I became sad; some tears came to my eyes. She reacted to this with quiet bafflement. Yet she did not immediately respond internally with the usual feeling that I wanted her to remain. She sensed correctly, although not fully, that my tears were an expression of sadness at the impending closing off of our relationship and that I wished her happiness and further growth.

What followed in the next few sessions was important. First, a stressful outside situation developed which she dared to discuss more openly than she had ever done before lest I would try to overprotect her and possess her. She also saw more clearly than ever before that she had been very guarded in most of her relatedness to me. I was further convinced by other data that trust was now emerging. Furthermore, there was genuine evidence of a sorting-out of issues that had to be solved realistically from those that reflected distortions of relationships.

There followed a very significant meeting with her father

in which she first recognized that she felt deeply neglected by him and that she did not dare to challenge his strange rationalizations for his unwillingness to express happiness over her excellent opportunity for her career. She also observed correctly that her peculiar irritation with her father was provoked by hints of real affection that he might have for her, usually blurred by childish preoccupations with incidental issues.

There was no question that the real analytic work had gotten under way following the unexpected expression of sadness by the analyst. It is also of interest that the patient recognized a real change in her engagement in the analysis but was not clear as to what had initiated it. This latter point offers interesting speculation on the patient's capacity to react while at the same time being unable to recognize the provocative components in the situation.

As we have attempted to point out with these clinical examples, the element of surprise operating in a serious concentrated interpersonal manifold seems conducive to novelty in the interpersonal patterns of reaction. At the moment of the surprise, neither participant had expected what would happen. In addition, the surprise by definition both avoids actual invasion of reality operations and/or utilizes age-old parataxic pathways of interaction.

The acting-out of the therapist appears to be an unconscious scanning response to the neurotic atmosphere communicated in subthreshold form to the analyst's receptive unconscious. We are purposely not regarding this acting-out as a counter-transference operation in the conventional sense. If the acting-out contacts the patient's past experience in neurotic interaction with others, then a laboratory situation has been created that closely resembles the actual conditions of the patient's living. An interpersonal set of appropriate coherence and perspective has been fashioned. The reconstruction-in-immediacy of a genuine laboratory problem in living increases the probability that something pertinent is being solved. Furthermore, one guards against structuring the patient-doctor relatedness as an exclusivistic twosome. Needless to say, although the doctor-patient relationship is one of a kind, it is not designed to wall off the patient from significant exploration in the outside world or to establish a cozy atmosphere which becomes virtually the patient's secret solution for avoiding challenge and uncertainty in the outside world.

The analytic situation is itself a great paradox. It must be so. It genuinely encourages the experiencing of universal tragedy and the sense of profound uncertainty which are the enduring aspects of all human existence. These existential qualities of man's human condition are unhypocritically, unmenacingly explored; they are explored without immediate need to act. In fact, to act may cause these inner experiences to vanish before they are grasped. This is the atmosphere which must be provided for the analytic situation.

The paradox is that the analyst must be operationally, in his very being, both different from and similar to the patient. Only when both elements of this paradox exist can emergence develop. If the analyst is basically so different and so out of touch with the intuited nuance components of the patient's neurosis (this has nothing to do with his scientific information about neurosis), the relatedness of doctor and patient is too bewildering, threatening, and distancing for the patient. Of course, if the doctor's counter-transference compliance cannot shed itself as the analysis proceeds, then nothing much happens in the analysis either. But we strongly suggest that, where many seasoned analysts fail, younger analysts succeed because they are closer to the unanalyzed core of their own problems and can recreate the *milieu intérieur* more naturally for traction with the patient. By seasoned we mean someone who does not need to react to the neurotic involvements of the patient. Hence the patient will have no respectable card of admission to the relationship. This view of the analyst's maturation is similar to what one observes in the learning process.

Clinically, we observe that the all-important neutrality of the analyst in the early experience in analysis can gradually give way to a more clearly defined emergence of individuality so that constructive nonidentity now can be constructive identity. Of course, this emergence is not arranged but should be an automatic prelogical field process. All behavior that is consciously designed to fit the situation is already insensitive, lacking in deeper contact, and artificial.

The question must be raised as to whether the therapist does not enter the parataxic areas of the patient's life much more often than he realizes, if he dares to recognize this. The distinction as to when this unconscious operation is of value and when it is not has to be explored further. One point that seems indisputable is that, once the intrusion is made, the therapist must be able to assume responsibility for his actions and thoughts with honesty and without defensiveness. The therapist probably avoids burdening the patient as long as the solution of his own problems of living is in good measure meaningful.

From our observation, it seems that counter-transference reactions are more likely to occur during fallow or lengthy resistant periods. They function at such times to provoke contact with the patient, to break into the resistance by surprise. The surprise is not a random juggling of the controls to see what will happen, but occurs in a setting of deep concentration in which the analyst is trying to reach the patient. The surprise is an expression of spontaneity, and as such can have constructive and unconstructive implications. The analyst must be free to follow through and participate in the truest sense of the word—there is no time at that point for sophistical defensive operations. His special responsibility at such a time is to recognize that he may be making irrational demands on the patient and that he must be able to handle this. It is not the patient's job to support him if his spontaneity creates tensions. Thus the utilization of counter-transference reactions in the treatment setting is not license to carry on irresponsible experimentation. If the therapist feels that he is playing with fire, he should not deal with counter-transference reactions with his patient; in other words, the optimal conditions for such exploration are not at hand.

If one wishes to appraise the possible injurious effects of exploring counter-transference reactions in the therapeutic situation, the only conceivable injury which requires serious consideration is that which could be imposed on the patient by the therapist's own attitude. If the therapist is serious, responsible, competent, and resourceful, it seems highly improbable that the patient will react with panic or a depression or that he will suddenly leave treatment. It is, moreover, significant that in our experience the examination of counter-transference reactions has not led to further bogging down and resistance. On the contrary, the more usual result has been the re-establishment of varying degrees of contact, further activity, and more hopefulness.

Historically, the fact that counter-transference reactions can be profitably utilized without causing undue distress has gained broader recognition. But the issue is one that deserves scientific scrutiny in the interests of more fruitful psycho-analytic procedures. Counter-transference can neither be disregarded because of its unfortunate derogatory connotations nor merely bravely faced in defense of one's own reactions. We suggest that these types of reaction need to be considered, not as an unwarranted and proscribed intrusion into the patient's field, but as a legitimate and valuable form of contact between therapist and patient through the prelogical mode of communication.

11

Some Observations on Dreams & Dream Analysis

RECENT physiological studies carried out on sleeping persons reveal that everyone probably dreams at intermittent intervals during sleep.[1] If a person awakes or is awakened during one of these intervals, he is able to recall dreaming. But if he awakes or is awakened during a quiescent interval, he may have no recollection of having dreamed. Thus it would seem that a great deal of dreaming is done even when it cannot be recalled on awaking.[2]

1] Nathaniel Kleitman, *Problems of Consciousness*, H. A. Abramson (ed.), Transactions of the Fifth Conference March 22–24, 1954, Macy Foundation, p. 113.
2] Parenthetically, it has been observed that numerous patients are able to report dreaming once they have entered therapy, in contrast to their alleged dreamless sleep previously. It seems that many persons can alert themselves to respond to internal and external signals if the conditions for such response are sufficiently urgent.

If it were practicable to awaken all "undreaming" patients in therapy

Furthermore, dreaming seems to be a homeostatic process. What do we mean by "homeostasis" in this connection? We are of the opinion that the dream phenomenon is evidence of spurts or showers of symbolizing activity occurring during the state of sleep. These symbolizing activities deal with the broad spectrum of the problems of man's existence. They reflect his passions, his vanities, his affects, his conceptions of himself and others. The syntax of these symbolizing activities can range from simple wish fulfillments to extraordinarily complex, undecipherable pictures. As man is constantly symbolizing during the waking state, it should not surprise us to recognize that this exclusively human phenomenon obtains even in sleep.

The traditional attitude toward the function of the dream has been to regard it as the guardian of sleep, as well as the means for the gratification of unconscious instinctual wishes. As we see it, these are merely special limited aspects of the dream function. It is highly questionable that they can be regarded as the *sine qua non* or necessary first cause of the dream. If dreaming is the guardian of sleep, it should occur whenever needed sleep is threatened with interruption; however, this is not the case. If dreams gratify unconscious instinctual wishes, why is it that so few dreams are obviously pleasurable? Perhaps we would not need to wish anyone pleasant dreams if dreams were usually pleasant.

Freud by-passes the dilemma implicit in the idea of instinctual gratification by alluding to the disguise inherent

---

during any one of the natural dream intervals, probably the "nondreaming" patient would be surprised by his dream. Probably also the therapist would be dissuaded from assuming that the patient's dreams are an ingratiating gift.

in the dream. Our objection to this view is not directed against the possibility that the dreamer is disguisedly carrying out an instinctual act, but against the gratuitous assumption that there is gratification present. Certainly in the waking state a great deal of instinctual activity need in no way be gratifying. Why should we infer that, because a person has a dream which on inference itself is of an instinctual nature, that particular instinctual act is gratifying? It seems unwise to apply a notion which by definition implies pleasure in its phenomenological sense to an experience in which the phenomenological component of pleasure is obviously lacking.

The unwarranted assumption of gratification, we believe, has two untoward consequences: first, it provides the therapist with the authority to assume a value judgment about the patient which could be erroneous and misleading and conducive to overlooking something undiscovered; second, in terms of the further expansion of psychoanalytic theory, it fails to distinguish clearly between observation and premise. The narrow emphasis on gratification blinds us to the recognition of a more extensive physiological requirement of man's existence, namely his symbolizing activity. This symbolizing activity is the very ground of man's human existence—there is no human existence apart from it.

One might say that a dream can never be interpreted by a patient; that is, that the observer, in the form of the analyst, has to interpret the dream. The patient, at best, produces very important information through the process of free association. The analyst gives to the unconscious and conscious material linkages which are not in their fullest meaning known to the patient; and, presumably not defensive about the data, he is able to make certain constructs out of it.

151

If by interpretation one simply means that more abstract inferences are drawn from the data, however, one quickly learns to recognize that it is the quality of these inferences, rather than their quantity, that determines their value. A valuable interpretation is one that assists the patient in obtaining a first clear confrontation of the way in which he relates himself to people. In other words, if thoroughly understood or at least if approximately understood, the dream frequently gives the patient a better conception of the way he feels about himself and the way he feels about other people. But really constructive interpretation involves even more than this. It is not simply exclusively confrontation. It must introduce novelty in the person's conception of himself so that he can increase the utilization of his inherent potential and equip himself to increase his learning capacities. Hence, a valuable dream interpretation not only increases the person's effective understanding of himself, but tends to release the learning powers which have been inhibited, thereby increasing the person's capacity to use his spontaneity to dare more in living, and so on. The interpretation might be geared directly to proving a particular theory, which with dexterity and ingenuity can be done; yet the patient has really learned very little about his true inner self and only has an illusory sense of new grasp.

The dream is in this respect the best projective technique available to us since it is completely unstructured by anyone except the patient and he can react to it freely as he would to a Rorschach or to other projective data, except that in this case the patient has created his own projective data. Freud considered the dream to be the royal road to the unconscious because the technique of free association required a minimum of encumbrance of conscious intervention; and since, naturally, the patient is not in touch with the meaning of the dream by virtue of its obscure symbology, he is much less tempted to restrict remarks or modify thoughts or block the emergence of material in any conscious sense. The patient's blocking is observed in changes of tempo, in talk, and in sudden divergences from an aspect of the dream that is being discussed, or perhaps in a sudden mood change. These changes indicate that unconscious material is coming to the surface and is being resisted. The dream can operate as resistance, and one of the technical problems presented to the analyst is to define when the data of association in connection with dreams are an expression of resistance in contrast to an expression of unconscious material. Freud very early recognized that patients' dreams were organized resistance to his interpretations. Dreams are often subtly organized to protect the individual in a way that duplicates the neurotic pattern of the waking state.

Freud made the important discovery that the dream message in many instances serves essentially to illuminate the patient's obstructionism. This obstructionism obtains first priority so that the meaning of the dream per se is then valueless. The patient is generally unaware that his dream is used as resistance, and he might stubbornly oppose such an interpretation by his therapist. Since the patient has no convincing clues to this misuse of the dream, it is only through the gathering of further tributary forms of resistance that he is persuaded to recognize the dream as a form of resistance. The resistance operates to preclude various significant data of a potentially threatening or damaging nature from entering the patient's awareness. The human peculiarity—that one resists and can be unaware of it—offers one of the most time-consuming, challenging problems to effective therapeutic interaction.

Most patients do have serious distrust of the interpretations in the beginning, and that distrust is not all irrational. We have to assume that basically the person's defenses are ubiquitous, and that they operate in a sense the way reflexes do. The defensive structure is something which is very stubbornly relinquished; the patient is constantly parrying with the analyst and trying to shadow-box himself out of a situation which might give him anxiety. This is just as automatic as the blinking of an eye when something comes close to it, except that in this situation the person does not even know that he is blinking.

This seemingly hopeless impasse calls for expansion of the analyst's latent grasp of the patient's unconscious so that, by surprise, he recovers a novel hunch about the patient, thereby giving new impetus to the relatedness with him. The therapist, as we see it, is obligated to utilize his unconscious resources in such a situation. This practical illustration establishes the grounds for insisting on the analyst's maximal utilization of all avenues of contact with a patient, even counter-transference responses, despite their discredited usefulness, contain wisdom.

One of the problems of analytic interpretation is that of avoiding incorporation of the interpretation of data into the defenses against insight. It requires constant ingenuity and novelty on the part of the analyst because as soon as he gets into a stereotyped way of thinking, whether in interpreting waking behavior or the dream, the patient immediately can cancel out any advantages from it. The process of analysis and dream interpretation as such should be a new unfolding throughout the analysis; this means that the creative process has to go on as long as the patient is in analysis. When the creative element diminishes, the analysis becomes less productive or clogged up. What this means is that the prelogical, subthreshold contact between the analyst and the patient no longer seems to produce any new insight. In terms of communication theory, one can say that the unconscious input of the patient is reduced. In other words, it can be assumed that if patient and analyst are operating effectively together, there is a continuously intermittent flow of certain kinds of data that can be of some constructive meaning.

As the analysis proceeds, it may be "jammed" by a specific set of interpretations. A characteristic type of interpretation may unwittingly block the further elaboration of unconscious data. Part of the need for novelty, creativity, and flexibility in analytic interpretations is to forestall what might be called, metaphorically, the chemistry of the mass-action reaction, where a particular set of ions accumulates too prodigiously and thus stops the chemical reaction from proceeding. This refers to processes occurring simultaneously in the analyst and in the patient. The patient may communicate new data perhaps, but no new information. Whatever additional data he brings to the analyst has no increased relevance; it does not add meaning to the context, to the formulation, or to the awareness of the relationship of himself to the analyst and to other important persons in his life, or to what has already been established between them.

Problems of transference and counter-transference mechanics influence the nature of dream material and often contribute to ineffectual utilization of the data by patient and analyst.

The problem of interpreting the dream, the patient's dream, is not just a problem of the patient's dream; the process involves two people, the patient and the analyst. Once the patient reports a dream, the meaning grows out of the shared experience on a nonverbal or prelogical level, since interpretation rests on a prelogical intuitive interaction of the patient and the analyst.

It is now well known that the symbology of the dream is partly cast in the context of the patient-therapist relationship. Many years ago, Wittels observed that the dreams of his patients tended in manifest content to contain pictorializations congenial to his own interests. His own interests had always been literary and poetic; his patients eventually dreamed in rather literary language and in poetic form. The idiom of the dream is attuned to the hearer of the dream.

Clinically, an important distinction has been made between first dreams that a patient dreams in the early interviews and dreams that are brought on later in the course of the therapy. Freud observed this and others have subsequently pointed out that the first dream or maybe even the first few dreams are perhaps more diagrammatic of the patient's whole life problem than anything that follows. Certainly they are less encumbered by the developing impact of the therapeutic relationship. The dream messages are now being influenced by new variables, namely the analytic experience and the doctor-patient relationship. These variables increase the complexity of dream interpretation but need not invalidate the process.

To sharpen the possible implication of the doctor-patient

relationship on the structuring of the dream, let us assume that the personality of the therapist always influences in some way the dream structure. Then let us seek to study its consequences. This raises the question whether the relationship to the analyst is so important that it must overshadow the individuality of the dream. Maybe this is a contradiction, for there is no exclusively individualistic dream totally isolated from contact with other persons; the dreamer is constantly in one sense or another relating himself to anybody he is in contact with, even if the relatedness is very remote. But since the patient tells his dreams during analysis more to his analyst than to anybody else, the dreams are structured in such a way that they reveal as much about the relationship to the analyst as they do about the relationship to other significant figures. The value of this is something that Freud neglected. He assumed that, to the extent that the analyst-patient relationship structured the dreams and the material of the analysis, it was an interference of negative value and something to be avoided by various techniques and maneuvers, which he elaborated and described in some detail.

But it might be in this, as it is in accredited scientific procedures, that to introduce a more complex artifact is only a virtual complication which, in reality, assists ultimately in the solution of the problem. The analyst represents many of the significant figures of the patient's past. The artifact is, first, that he is not these people and, second, that his own personality attributes are completely irrelevant to the patient's program of living but indispensable to the analytic work.

To anticipate a new or novel development in the theory

of dream interpretation, one might have to suspect that conventional dream interpretation only goes so far. It may be valid up to a point, but we must first demonstrate in what way it fails and on that basis explore new possibilities that have so far been neglected in traditional dream theory and consequently in the established procedures of dream analysis.

In the classical approach to the dream, the central technique focuses on creating a milieu of minimal resistance so that the latent meaning of the dream will emerge through free association. The giftedness of the analyst and his subtlety of observation play a very important role in this classical method. He must hear, for example, slight changes in intonation, in the pacing of the communication of the patient, and he must recognize that these might have a meaning. In fact, hesitations, repetitions of dreams, and omissions alert him to deeper material. He points out these characteristics to see what comes of it. But if the resistances are too powerful, the analyst's skill will be of little avail. Experience shows that many patients anticipate patterns of interpretation dealing with only a few possibilities, e.g., dependency wishes, castration anxiety, and so on. Repetition of interpretation sets a precedent in the patient's mind. He thinks, "Oh, sure, I know what is going to happen; the next set of dreams will show that I am afraid of my father, a thing I knew anyway." Thus a circumscribed overdetermined patterning of interpretation can become itself an obstruction to progress.

To reach through the patient's resistances to the deeper material, constant flexibility has to be maintained in interpretation. The element of novelty has to be maintained. The dreams which have a gross similarity have to be tackled afresh each time. The repetition pattern of the dream reveals an unresolved message. A shift of emphasis is called for, and not merely a paraphrasing of an old interpretation.

Utilization of a broader band of unconscious contact with the patient provides a more legitimate prognostic criterion for the therapeutic enterprise. We are all confronted with the question of the analyzability of patients; although we do not have rigorous criteria on which to depend for prognosis, we have to be as sure as we can that we have come to the most probably correct appraisal of the prognostic picture. To mention one extreme, if we are essentially inert as therapists, and if the patient is not responding to therapy, are we clear in assuming a poor prognosis? Certainly for that specific illustration the prognosis is poor, but the underlying limitation might be in the mode of therapy rather than in the patient. If, on the other hand, we feel convinced that we have utilized the full spectrum of our capacities, the difficulty can reasonably be appraised as residing either in our specific limitations with a specific patient or in the patient's inability to respond to therapy. The first conclusion would lead us to recommend to the patient further therapy with someone else; the second could lead us to recommend cessation of treatment. In either case, we must give the patient our honest appraisal of what his hopes for health are as far as we can judge the matter.

One searches for a method of obviating the kind of interpretive pitfall one gets into whenever a theory about human beings is too circumscribed. The theory of personality itself conditions the interpretation of a dream. It is helpful certainly; but since any theory has limitations, one tries to understand these limitations lest they take command of the empirical situation and cause it to bog down. The theory of personality used in the interpretation of the dream orders the data of the dream and organizes the possible inferences from the dream. What was once fresh becomes habitual, what was once novel may become clichéd, and a useful endeavor stagnates.

To construct a theoretical system that transcends theoretical systems is itself a paradox. In the history of psychoanalysis there have been few really great constructs other than Freud's. Dreams have been interpreted through the centuries in various ways—as manifestations of instinctual forces, as prophecy and psychic revelations, as ethical reflections, and so on. We may suspect, therefore, that other dynamic elements modify the effective use of even the best theory of dream interpretation. Freud has quite correctly pointed out that associative material presented by the patient in an easy-flowing manner is usually preconscious material and that it is through the hesitations, the embarrassments, the divagations revelatory of resistance that one is led to the important deeper layers of the personality.[3] But he has perhaps too narrowly defined the nature of this preconscious material and too rigidly circumscribed the procedures to be employed in bringing it into emergence.

The interpretive value of dreams has been questioned by antagonists of dream theories who claim that the dream life, in effect, is a specious product, a result produced as an hypnotic effect of the analyst on the patient. The analyst merely recaptures the reflections of his own theories without

3] See Sigmund Freud, *Collected Papers* (New York: Basic Books, 1959), Volume 5, chapters 12 and 13.

realizing it. Freud attempted to meet this challenge. In this connection he tells of a young man, a tenacious doubter at every turn, who had beautifully confirmatory dreams. Freud raises the question as to whether the confirmatory dreams are merely evidence of compliance; compliance here refers to the unconscious need of the patient to submit to the authority of the analyst in such a way that the scientific validity of the dream material as an indicator of the patient's emotional attitudes is obscured. Freud's task is to demonstrate that the patient's dream material validly establishes his interpretation and that it is not solely an expression of unconscious acquiescence.

If there is significant unconscious need for compliance, then the complexity of the situation is so increased that the task of establishing the correctness of the analyst's interpretation becomes virtually impossible. Part of this obstruction to the solution is due to the fact that the unconsciously compliant acquiescent attitude of the patient creates by its very nature a set inappropriate to scientific inquiry. Certainly it is an indication that the patient is not collaborating in the search for the truth. Thus one cannot anticipate any effectual attack on the problem by turning to the compliant patient for assistance.

This illustration given by Freud suggests primarily that the strongly negativistic character make-up of the patient allows him the luxury of supreme compliance since he can always protect himself from insight by his doubts. The manifest dreams in such instances are good examples of the defensive components of the character since they re-emphasize the similarities of the dream state and the waking state.

Perhaps at our present stage of experience with dream

material and dream interpretation, so-called confirmatory dreams may either confirm what is going on, fail to do so, or open up new areas of exploration. There are a number of uses to which the so-called confirmatory dream can be put aside from attempting to confirm anything.

Sometimes the patient can be shown that the dream illustrates at best only virtual contact with the analyst and others and that the poorness of contact is concealed from the patient by a seeming relatedness. This type of relatedness avoids friction and maintains amicability. In such a way the confirmatory dream itself can become the means for studying important aspects of the patient's character. In fact, the dream is confirmatory on the ground that the behavior of the patient in the analysis confirms the dream, rather than that the dream has to confirm the analyst's interpretation.

Something broader than compliance is operating in many of these cases and therefore has significant implications if properly viewed. For example, we all know that in ordinary conversation we arrange our communications purposively so that we will be understood. If one thinks of conditions in which a person has some special need *not* to be understood, is attempting seriously to mislead another person, we are naturally dealing with a different state of affairs. But let us assume that two persons are genuinely concerned with understanding the topic being discussed. And, therefore, that unwittingly processes operate whereby the patient makes his ideas and feelings known to the analyst in a language or dream symbology which might make it easier for the analyst to understand him. If it is assumed that all apparent compliance is neurotic whenever the patient borrows the language, phrasing, or viewpoint of the analyst, whether in the pictorial symbols of dreams or in the verbal interchange, the natural or inherent striving of human beings to communicate meaningfully is then overlooked. In addition, as has often been observed, one of the real advantages of the psychotherapeutic setting is that, unfortunately for the first time in some cases, the patient is seriously listened to. The analyst asks questions and makes remarks which reveal a sincere interest in understanding what the patient is talking about. It might not be extravagant then to expect that the patient in turn will wish to communicate to the analyst what he is struggling with, despite the all too familiar phenomenon of resistance.

The question of the written dream must also be touched upon in an examination of dream analysis. Freud took the position that a dream should not be written down: "Although a patient may attempt to overcome his forgetting of his dreams by writing them down as soon as he awakens, we can tell him that it is useless to do so because the resistance in which he may preserve the text of the dream will transfer itself to the associations and thereby render the manifest content of the dream inaccessible for interpretation."[4]

In a recent discussion of the written dream, Lipschutz describes it as "a much overdetermined typical piece of acting-out." Abraham and Sharp, whom he cites, also regard it as a transference dream, a highly invested narcissistic product, a symbolic gift; they also emphasize its anal aspect on the basis of their observations in clinical experience. Most analysts do not encourage the writing of dreams, or ignore

4] Lipschutz, "The Written Dream," *J. Amer. Psychoan. Assoc.*, II, 473–78.

the written dream if it is brought to them. As Lipschutz rightly points out, however, psychoanalysts must regard with interest and curiosity every aspect of the patient's behavior.[5] The writing of dreams during analysis is not an unusual occurrence, and the analyst is frequently presented with this form of behavior.

Lipschutz interestingly presents, side by side, the verbal and written reports of a patient's dream. He had the patient first give his verbal recall without the assistance of the written report and then read out his written report. The verbal report, Lipschutz points out, is a clearer statement of the situation than the written report, which is a somewhat disguised presentation of the material.

The verbal report of one such dream is as follows: "I am getting dressed in girl's clothes somewhere. I don't know how the fellows will take it. So I change back feeling disappointed." The written report reads: "I get all dressed in girl's clothes, but I feel it isn't being received well by the fellows. So I put on my own clothes and feel relieved."

Lipschutz points out the contradiction between the two reports: "In the verbal dream the feeling is one of disappointment at having to change back because it is doubtful how the fellows, 'analyst,' will take it. In the written dream the feeling is one of relief." Although he is correct in the literal observation of the contradiction, the fundamental meaning of the dream is not altered at all. For example, in the verbal report one gets the notion that the patient is

---

5] Wilhelm Stekel, in *Interpretation of Dreams, New Developments and Technique* (New York: Liveright, 1943), also makes the same point. Actually, he not only did not object to the writing down of dreams; he often instructed his patients to write down every dream.

stating that there is something in himself which makes him feel that he would like to be a woman, or to submit, or something of that order; but he then begins to recognize that the fellows, as he puts it, might have an adverse reaction to his being a female. So he feels disappointed, which means that he is being obstructed from playing out something that he would like to play out. In the written report, again, one sees that he is all dressed up in girl's clothes, which must represent that in some way there is something about such a role that is important to him and appealing to him. But again he is confronted with the fact that the outside world, perhaps the analyst too, would not countenance or accept his acting out his female role, so he quickly changes back to the acceptable role and feels relieved that he has not been discovered.

The written dream, if anything, more minutely shows the extreme importance to this man of not revealing to others some of his private cherished wishes that would not fit in with the community. In the verbal report one does not recognize the extent to which he may find it imperative not to disclose his unconscious wishes or, let us say, his unconscious desire to experience the feminine role. The author shows, as have others, that one can profitably utilize both the written and the verbal report of the dream. When a dream is recalled, one assumes that resistance will be present and show up in the associations. Why then regard the very transparent resistance expressed by the act of writing down the dream as necessarily insuperable?

An important observation for therapeutic and theoretic purposes is that much of what occurs in the dream is seen to occur in the waking state of the patient's relationships with other people. The defensive qualities of the waking state are very frequently reduplicated in a pattern in the dream. The manifest content of the dream may differ widely in a literal way from the content of the waking state. However, the connection between the two is not particularly obscure, and from the practical standpoint it is often helpful to have the patient recognize that the same defensive patterns operate in the waking state as in the dream state. An appreciation of this fact tends to help him see the possibility of rational connections between different states of consciousness.

For example, one day a particular patient blocked during the hour, found herself unable to think of anything, and became visibly embarrassed and ill at ease. She turned on the analyst and in a semi-joking, flirtatious manner suggested that since she had nothing to say, maybe he would say something. She continued to make a number of harmless, jibing remarks intended to reduce the tension produced by the blockage. The analyst, under the circumstances, preferred at this particular time to sit quietly and see what would happen.

The next day the patient told of two occurrences that she thought might be of importance. One was a real experience with her husband. She had apparently forgotten to prepare a late meal for him and when he confronted her with this with some disapproval, although not in any particular anger, she became extremely frightened, much more so than she could account for. Her way of dealing with this state of tension was to become somewhat argumentative and snide in her manner, disowning responsibility and attempting to make the husband feel that he was exaggerating the difficulties to which she subjected him.

That night she had a dream in which her father and a number of male relatives—all similar to the distorted stereotype of her father, namely, rather domineering, powerful figures to her—had released some gas from a stove in the room where she was. She became very frightened and searched quickly for her daughter so that they could escape. At the height of the anxiety she awakened. Her first association was an amusing childhood experience with her mother which had to do with flatus; the mother would occasionally pass gas and then joke with her children, telling funny little stories about it and pretending that they must find out who had passed the gas.

In these illustrations the patient was unable to capture the minute elements leading up to the blocking in the analytic hour or in her relationship to her husband. She sensed in herself a vague note of defiance at that moment but also got exaggeratedly frightened as if something dreadful would happen to her for thwarting her analyst and her husband. She dealt with the dangerous situation by an assortment of maneuvers such as joking, flirting, counter-accusations, impertinence, and silliness. She was unable to identify anything that was going on beyond the registration in her of the other's alleged "fury and impatience" with her, which she attempted to ward off by these maneuvers.

In the treatment situation it became increasingly evident to the therapist that inexplicable episodes of fear and tension followed even minimal challenges in adaptation. It was imperative for the patient *not* to recognize the existence of the challenge, partly because of deeply rooted resentment and bitterness plus great self-loathing for her sense of helplessness. Thus the phenomenal behavior was one in which the presenting phase was that of floundering fear followed by an assortment of responses stifling to inquiry. These consisted of silliness, impertinence, and grievous reproaches against the therapist. The association of the childhood experience with her mother followed wakening and was a similar process for dealing with the mysterious and alarming dream experience. Matters that should seriously concern her merely overpowered her with panicky feelings, after which a whole string of ineffectual and obnoxious defenses were called into play to salvage her composure. She reacted to responsibility as though some destructive claim was made on her or she was being brutally victimized by the person towards whom she felt responsible.

In this investigation, one must keep in mind the fact that our interest is that of the psychiatrist. This makes a particular context for all the communications that go on. Keeping this point in mind might lead to less unnecessary confusion between the different scientific disciplines in their attack on the nature of the dream or in their use of the dream as a tool; the anthropologist, psychologist, psychiatrist, and others use the dream with somewhat different intentions. There is no reason why one must assume that the same self-evident end point will be achieved. In fact, one might assume quite the contrary. Scientists of different disciplines who feel that they ought to come to identical conclusions really miss the point of their own contribution. Instead of recognizing that each of the different disciplines might throw light on a particular area, they erroneously assume that the validity of the final results is only established by complete congruence.

This type of misconception must be dispelled. If the same discipline is used, then one must assume that lack of verification indicates that something is wrong; but if different disciplines are used, a lack of immediate verification cannot be said, *ipso facto,* to establish some fallacy on the part of either discipline. It probably means that there is not sufficient over-all scientific coordination of the project. The investigators in one discipline tend to be somewhat suspicious of the other disciplines and to discredit probably essentially valid materials coming from them. For example, the existence of the unconscious is hotly disputed even today—not, however, in psychoanalytic circles, where there is a commonly experienced deep understanding of the subject derived from clinical work. If one works with patients, one must come to the general conclusion that there is a phenomenon evidenced by these patients which has gone under the rubric of dissociated data. The dissociative process has been observed by all schools of psychiatry. But then, when the process is discussed, the discussants can involve themselves in metaphors, reifications, blatant logical inconsistencies, and invalid fictions.

Yet the cause is not really lost. The tremendous revolutionary developments in physics did not militate against its growth because its weaknesses were within the intra-disciplinary frame of reference and were not inter-disciplinary. Truly inter-disciplinary research has the formidable task of creating a common frame of reference which is at least partially given in the intra-disciplinary setting.

12

The Dream as a Message

AN APPRAISAL of psychoanalytic dream interpretation suggests that the methodology of physical science is not adequate for a productive grasp of the meaning and significance of dreams. A great deal of what goes on in man is not expressed in the logical forms employed in science but in forms that are commonly considered non-logical. These aspects of experience need to be placed into a communicational form that will enable one to deal with them in a nonmystical fashion without burdening the analysis with dry and limiting artifacts imposed by exclusively logical formulations. The ideas and feelings connected with dream material are often extremely difficult to put into simplified scientific vocabulary. As distressing as it might be to persons of a narrowly scientific bent, metaphor has a very important position in the constructive analysis of dreams.

The dream appears to express man's way of organizing life

experience and his inner reflection of himself in a symbology which he quickly casts off as soon as he awakens. Thus it does not lend itself to immediate logical operational inference. It can be seen, however, as a complex set of cues and signals which appear to the dreamer primarily in pictorial form. The dreamer's personality structure as well as the dream process makes inaccessible a full appreciation of all the implications of the dream. In telling the dream, the patient describes his life situation; and he describes not only what he experiences in awareness, but much more than he is aware of. The peculiar wisdom of the dream, inscrutable as it may appear, often transcends man's waking knowledge of himself.

But for the experience to be fully fruitful, one must approach the dream through the prelogical, intuitive mode of thinking and feeling in which it is experienced. The therapist must use his creative unconscious spontaneously, rather than applying a fixed theory of what the dream means. There are very real advantages, we believe, to regarding the dream as a metaphysical statement of a problem-solving issue, as an attempt to say something about one's way of life and about one's conception of one's self as a human being. By limiting the interpretation of dreams to the resolution of certain instinctual problems, one tends to underestimate man's understanding of himself and the human situation, be it unconscious or even preconscious.

The dream is man's most blatant paradox, with its shameless absurdities, its utter disregard of common sense, its violation of so much of the treasured wisdom of the waking state. But—another paradox—it can reveal to man great truths sometimes more powerfully and compactly than the most eloquent confrontation. What man perceives out of awareness is often truer and richer than what he perceives in awareness with all his cognitive processes in operation. A rigid adherence to scientific method in dream analysis has tended to obscure this complex paradoxical quality of dreams.

Most communications in the therapeutic setting are also highly paradoxical in nature; and the statement of a paradox is often the beginning of a fruitful discourse. The patient very often makes a statement which he believes to be a simple statement of what is going on. But the therapist recognizes that this communication is indeed a much more complex and contradictory one than it appears to be on the face of it and that the patient must be guided to a realization of this fact.

The problem is not one of deciding from all the contradictory elements presented that A is the right solution and B is wrong. The point is that the paradox is not really a proposition that can be verified or denied. On the contrary, its nature is metaphysical. As such, it simply poses a problem. It calls attention to an area of experience to be further investigated. In the course of this investigation, problems can be defined and propositions formulated in a way that permits them to be verified or denied. For example, in the therapeutic interview, the patient may say that he loves his wife, and this statement may seem to be a pure statement of fact. Yet there may be correlative evidence that the matter is not quite so simple. Some verbal intonation, gesture, or inflection signals to the therapist that there is inherent in the statement a lurking paradox, an underlying doubt. This marks it as an area for investigation.

The Dream as a Message

Now in the course of analytic work, as the patient's life situation and problems emerge more and more in the analytic interchange, many contradictory and illogical statements come to light. It is often tempting to treat these things literally and to try to get rid of them, but we can see that they are the kernel of the individual's growth and development. What today is a self-contradictory or illogical statement is really the seed of what tomorrow is an intuition or an insight into the problems inherent in the life situation. This is especially true in dealing with material of dreams. Elements in the dream that are contradictory are often the germinal element of a new larger grasp of the life situation. Freud, in pointing out how the individual tries to protect himself in his dreams by means of censorship, perhaps has gone too far in emphasizing the disguising aspect of some of the apparent contradictions, such as a young person standing for an old person and other such polarities. Many of these things may really be the beginning of a formulation about a problematic situation rather than simply a disguised expression.

The essential point to recognize is that the material produced in analytic sessions frequently reveals repeated paradoxical situations, paradoxical attitudes, paradoxical feelings. These paradoxes have often been regarded by psychoanalysts as evidences of ambivalence. The inherent assumption is that there is a special type of end result that has to be achieved in order to resolve the ambivalence. The end result is often determined by the cultural position of the analyst. Let us say, for example, that in the setting of the family the assumption is that the parents and the children will always be able to get along; therefore, if the patient has ambivalent feelings toward a particular parent, these are supposed to come to the surface during analysis and then vanish in some sort of way, enabling him to fit himself into the cultural tradition of getting along. Actually, exploration of the paradoxes might reveal that our conceptions of man could stand some re-examination. A basically different conception of man— one, let us say, that is based on the inviolable aspects of man's feeling structure—might lead to a quite different resolution of the ambivalence that is met with in the therapeutic situation. In philosophical questions the paradoxes are very frequently studied from the standpoint of their illogicality; as soon as the premises are clarified, one can move from a somewhat confused state of affairs to a new and novel problem which offers further development. In the human situation during therapy, the same thing would be expected. However, man's behavior becomes significantly different when he is confronted with his loneliness, his fears of isolation, and other types of basic anxiety. These profound issues preclude any expectation of simple resolution through logical analysis alone.

Paradoxes are frequently not observed because they can remain well concealed behind the propositional form of a communication. The pictorial quality of the dream raises a peculiarly significant problem with respect to translating the dream into language for purposes of interpretation. Visual representation, as Rapaport points out, has the following real shortcomings in terms of logical verbal communication: (1) It is wanting in means to express relationships; (2) it is limited to either positing or not positing a content, and has only sparse means to qualify positing; (3) it lacks means to express abstractions; and (4) it is implicative or condensing, a quality which defies ordered verbal communication.[1]

Freud and others who have followed him have recognized that the particles of speech which determine the meaning of sentences cannot be communicated in any of the usual senses in the dream. The dream makes use of visual imagery to convey its message. But by means of the devices of repetition and the use of opposites and contrasts, the dream permits one to infer probable relationships of the dream "clauses." The various syntactical connections which the interpreter supplies to define meanings of ideas in dream material are inferences arising from his response to the dream.

Let us take, for example, a dream in which a person is locked up in a large building which, he observes, is surrounded by guards of some sort. As the dream progresses, this person is able to escape from the guarded place with no particular difficulty. Now in converting this dream picture into language, one could formulate it like this: "Even though the place is heavily guarded, the imprisoned person is nevertheless able to escape." One supplies, from inference, the conjunctive forms "even though" and "nevertheless." But there are also various other possible formulations. One could say, "If I leave this place, nobody will oppose my leaving," or "Even though these people surround the building and act as if they were guards, there is no opposition to my leaving." In other words, the grammatical syntax is determined only after one has responded as a whole to the manifest content of the dream.

In the conventional form of dream interpretation the

1] David Rapaport, *Organization and Pathology of Thought* (New York: Columbia University Press, 1951), p. 468, n. 39.

manifest content is structured from the particular way in which the pictorial symbols appear. Furthermore, the process of eliciting the manifest content of the dream which permits the dreamer, through free association, to come to the daily residue is actually similar to establishing the referents for each particular symbol of the dream. Then the latent meaning of the dream is arrived at through various types of resistances that begin to make themselves known at least to the therapist if not to the patient. The assumption is that if the person is permitted to talk in an atmosphere of minimum censorship, the accumulation of discursive components will eventually bring the deeper meaning of the dream to the surface. Thus one concentrates his attention upon the obvious discursive elements in the dream.

On the other hand, we propose, one could simply listen to the dream as one would listen to a piece of poetry and react immediately to it in the sense of its being a presentational experience or an intuitional type of experience. In listening to a dream by either approach, one does not usually accept the manifest content as if it were a literal statement; therefore, when one interprets the dream, one really abstracts the dream. The degree of abstracting that is done depends upon the complexity of the dream; or put otherwise, the abstraction process might be a rather simple one in certain types of dreams and an extremely complex one in others. In actual practice, if a dream states a particular proposition which is in the therapist's theory, then the manifest content of the dream is likely to be accepted at its face value. For example, if the patient dreamed that he had had intercourse with his mother, this dream might be taken as a literal statement of an obvious wish fulfillment; while if, on the other hand, there were other dreams which were equally clear in their presentation, one might be obliged to recognize that the dream could be equivalent to saying that this is just what one could say in consciousness but one would go on to look for the hidden meaning in the dream. The extent to which the hidden meaning is searched for is, of course, of some importance and must be dictated fundamentally by the assumption of the theory that is being used.

The dream is a message. What one does with the message is the vital issue. If one, so to speak, cripples the message and does not permit it to express its meaning, then one has done the dream a disservice. If one regards the dream as having communicated solely a simple fact, which in itself does not stimulate or excite both the dreamer and the listener to further areas of feeling and thought, then the dream has been misused. A great deal of difficulty with dream interpretation does not reside with the dream but with the people who discuss the dream. The dream has inherently an unending possibility of further mutual exploration by the dreamer and the therapist. Any type of interpretation, then, which would tend to produce a closure of the forward movement is already operationally a disservice to the dream. The dream must be approached with an attitude that permits and encourages further understanding of emotional experience. Often the errors in dream interpretation are not tactical errors but attitudinal errors; the interpreter is attempting to understand the dream as if he were simply decoding a message of purely factual content when, in reality, the dream cannot be looked upon quite that simply even though there are factual statements inherent in its total message. The interpretation must always aim to expand the meaning of the dreamer's life and not merely to make some flat-footed statement such as: he solely wants this or he wants that.

The message of the dream can be deciphered by the process of listening carefully and allowing the dream story to evoke images in the minds of the listeners. Different parts of the dream stimulate different fragmentary thoughts about the dreamer. One of the most striking discoveries one can make is the discovery of the pattern of dominant defensive operations in the waking state. In fact, under some conditions one might say that even the core problem, that is, the false solution to one's living, is posed. The patterns of relatedness to men and to women is often strongly hinted at. On numerous occasions, the intuitive response to the dream material suggests the existence of a psychosis or a homosexual orientation. We have been able to indicate what the patient's operations are with others although predicting the adaptive experience of the patient does not seem possible to arrive at. Thus, for example, if the patient is a person who continually presents himself as a victim and subtly induces others to feel guilty in their handling of him, these data will appear in some fashion in the manifest content of the dream. However, the patient's adaptive experience with respect to these phenomena may show no correlation. In other words, the patient would not know that he was acting out the role of the victim nor would he be aware of provoking guilt in others.

It is our opinion that the therapist who attempts to understand the meaning of dreams must be able to accept the challenge of understanding the other person's presentation of himself. With this in mind, we believe that a seminar on dream interpretation can help to develop the therapist's grasp and contact with the patient's problems of living. Such a seminar is conducted in a way that the therapists are forced to listen to the initial dream of a patient and are obliged to free associate to the manifest content of this dream, with the aim of divining the ways in which this patient is attempting to solve the problems of his life. It is important to emphasize here the freedom of expression that the therapists should have in their comments. Any argumentation or special pleading for a particular point of view is discouraged; contradictions and apparent absurdities of statements are respected. This respect for and encouragement of the variety of genuine responses leads to an atmosphere of minimal anxiety and defensiveness. The sense of immediacy is what is sought for; therefore, calculated, reasoned appraisals tend to be discouraged.

Is it possible for us, by responding to the manifest content of the dream, to anticipate what the person will present of himself to the world? Can the core problem, the central focus or false solution of this man's existence, be identified? Does the dream give clues as to how the person relates to men in contrast to women? Can the dream help us as to whether a psychosis or borderline psychotic condition is present?

Let us try through the variety of personal responses to the dream to see if a hunch may develop that points to the nature and severity of psychopathology. There is something we are responding to in the dream that genuinely indicates the nature of the patient's illness. The dream, like a poem, has potentially great evocative capabilities. Its presentational form transcends the limitations of its literal verbal content.

It is very important to identify, if possible, what are the

facts and what are the conditions that permit of successful dream analysis. It is just as important whether we succeed or not to get some idea of what spells success or failure.

The therapist who reports a case to the seminar must have it clearly in mind to meet the challenge of the group's responses to it. It is conceivable that these responses may include material that has not yet emerged in the analysis.

In presenting the responses to the dream, we must remember that it is more important to identify them truly than to be right. This spirit of freedom encourages the emergence of responses which will be in part overlapping but which also will be unique to the particular therapist's own emotional experience. It is very important that this spirit of freedom and integrity prevail.

Although in a positive sense one would be eager to grasp the patient's human problems through the medium of understanding his dreams, a more basic problem that is presented to us is the discovery of the parameters involved. By parameters we mean an attempt to discover not only what is knowable but also what is unknowable. Thus, for example, in our interpretation of the initial dream we have been amazingly astute in verifying defensive operations but we have been so far strikingly unsuccessful in predicting the patient's adaptive capacities. In clinical work it would be of the greatest value if we could understand why some persons whose psychopathology is so serious are still able to make an effective adjustment in their living, while others whose psychopathology is not so severe are practically crippled. So far as we can determine at present in our encounter with one another we cannot predict a patient's effectiveness in adaptation or adjustment from his dream.

To illustrate this we shall describe a report of a dream and the responses of the seminar to it. After the seminar has responded, there is an evaluation by the presenter who has had the patient at least a year or a year and a half in treatment. In that way the responses of the members of the seminar can be checked by the material of the therapist.

This is the initial dream reported to the presenting therapist by a twenty-five-year-old man:

> *I was in a railroad station. It had a very funny name— Shaffrus. I was waiting for a train when a Negro boy came by; he was naked. I was very surprised. I was going to ask him about his nakedness when the train passed full speed without stopping. The Negro boy told me then what I could do—run to the next station and catch it, which I started to do, feeling helpless about ever coming to catch up with the train.*

The following quoted remarks are the immediate responses of the eight members of the seminar to this dream. They know nothing else about the patient.

> *"He missed the boat!"*
> *"This is a wonderful dream!"*
> *"He is coming to the realization that life is passing him by and he can't catch up with it. The Negro boy represents his instinctual or primitive self which he has ignored in his life. He has been a very practical and limited intellectual person who has inhibited his legitimate, aggressive impulses."*
> *"He is not at home in the railroad station of his life."*
> *"Maybe he is a European?"*
> *"Rus means soot in German. Schaff means work or create."*
> *"The German word for conductor is Shaffner."*
> *"Catching a train by running after it is a sheer impossibility.*

It is something to be sorry for like a missed opportunity that can't be recaptured such as nursing at a breast."

"*The strange railway station may be the analyst's office.*"

"*It may express his feeling about the analysis.*"

"*The nakedness of the Negro boy may indicate his surprise at the possibility of being nakedly honest and direct. He was going to ask about it when the train rushed by.*"

"*The Negro boy could be childishness—something regressive or primitive. To play with a Negro boy is a self-indulgence which he is stuck with. He is lacking resources and is dependent on the boy.*"

"*He sees the world as a strange alien place; he tries to inquire but he is stopped by his ambition. In the dream he is showing himself how futile this is. The train symbolizes ambition. Catching the train is the practical goal, the thing to do. These goals are set for him, practical and ambitious goals set for him by other people. He can't stop to find out.*"

"*Shaffrus is a meaningless name, nonsense. It is closed at both ends by the letter s; it doesn't do anything or go anyplace.*"

"*Analysis makes him naked. He wants the impossible from analysis.*"

"*He is there on time but the train does not stop for him. Maybe that is the way he sets it up in his life.*"

"*Shaff means sheep. Black sheep. There is a real possibility he may be homosexual.*"

"*Let's consider it as a picture. There are two views: (1) the train is the most important part; (2) the Negro boy represents the central problem.*"

"*I think this man's stating that he has been so preoccupied with his own body or with sex in some way that he has let everything slip by him. The notion of Negro implies something derogatory in his mind about this. Desperation is ex-*

pressed by his missing the train and feeling hopeless. I suspect that he can't communicate openly in the analysis his hopelessness and his pathological preoccupation with sex and dirtiness. He is thinking about sex all the time. This may be manifest in the analysis or not. He feels desperate, in the clutches of this thing."

"He is not living up to the standards set, so he is a black sheep."

"It may be important that there are no women in the dream."

The presenter then discussed his experience with the patient:

"This dream was presented to me by the patient after many years of therapy with another psychiatrist. The patient was very preoccupied with what went wrong with this other psychiatrist. He had many feelings that he never told this psychiatrist. His associations to the word *Shaffrus* were—Schrafft's and Russo (my name). He had the feeling that he should buy some Schrafft's chocolates and eat them during the analytic hour. He was feeling exposed like the Negro boy and that he was being pressed too much.

"The presenting problems were the interruption of his treatment with the other psychiatrist, his work situation, and his relationship with his girl friend. His father did all his homework for him; and he felt always that he had to make his father happy; his father has had an empty life living for the boy. His mother was extremely neglectful of him and of the home. She was very sociable, played bingo all the time, and left him with the servants. He was filled with rage at her and her façade. He worked his way through school. In the second year of college he had a nervous breakdown. A year later he suffered a second breakdown and began the relationship with his previous psychiatrist. Afterward, he continued to work fairly successfully. He does not see his work goals as his own, and he has postponed advancement many times.

"The diagnostic impression is that of borderline psychosis with several clear psychotic episodes. The patient sought constant reassurance. He hides his psychopathology well. He is very fluent and charming socially. But he is aware of being very insincere and of malingering, of being an entertainer without any involvement with anybody.

"He gets in situations in which he is masochistic in life and sadistic in fantasy. He has all the perversions in his fantasy—voyeuristic, pedophilic, sadistic, and homosexual. He has symptoms of depersonalization and estrangement from reality.

"He sees the goal of advancing in his field as something imposed on him.

"He is a very handsome man, very careful about his hair and so on. He despises his concern about his body. He pursues heterosexual relationships and is something of a lady-killer. His girl friend is attentive and protective, and he is very helpless with her. He represses his hostility. He is very afraid of her getting angry with him if he dates other girls.

"Everybody who knows him has no idea of the extent of his psychopathology. He is very well thought of. He has a very good position in his field."

What has the seminar missed in responding to this dream? They missed his successful behavior with other people. They missed how the patient actually behaves in the outer world.

What has been captured? We have really recognized the

intense disturbance in this man's inner life—so much anxiety relating to his body and dirtiness; so preverbal that he cannot share it with anyone; not accessible because he is lost in the category of me, I, and myself. We have also captured his intellectual repressed aggression, his sense of being in a strange alien world, his feeling of futility, his self-indulgence, his evasiveness, and his preoccupations with sex and its derogatory implications for him.

The exploration of the dream with its demand on our deeply intuitive processes is counterbalanced by the demands of reality which oblige us to pay close attention to what man actually does with his life. Both the presentational and discursive processes require dedicated attention by therapist and patient alike. The dangers are that the therapist may become so involved in the dream world as to neglect reality or that the therapist is so out of touch with himself that he maintains an exclusively "reality"-oriented, literal-minded, manipulative, adaptive approach. There are also those who sacrifice the depth and range of their spontaneity to maintain the consistency of a discursive, logical, theoretical system. We are arguing against a premature intervention of discursive processes. In other words, the spontaneous response must be allowed to develop its full range before submitting to discursive criticism.

The meaning of the dream is constructively facilitated when the clinical atmosphere is emotionally constructive and stimulating. Similarly, in sharing with students the understanding of poetry, the great teacher does not simply make a propositional interpretation of the poem; he helps the student to release himself so that he may be able to reach into himself and move toward the meaning of the poem. The underlying unity or ground of this entire work on symbolism and dreams, the root of the tree, is the concept of a generative or fertile communication. The generative idea is not closed, not repetitive, nor inhibitive of expression and change. More positively, it is what we call a genuine expression of a human individual—a genuine communication of his experience. And perhaps what makes such an expression, such a communication, both genuine and generative is the wholeness of the individual's involvement in the communication. The entire experience of this person is at one with the expression, with the symbolic form; and this wholeness of engagement and of continuity is also the openness of the individual to growth and expansion.

INDEX